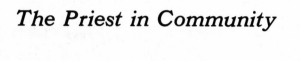

The Priest in Community

– *URBAN T. HOLMES, III*

THE PRIEST IN COMMUNITY
Exploring the Roots of Ministry

A CROSSROAD BOOK
The Seabury Press, New York

1978
The Seabury Press
815 Second Avenue
New York, N.Y. 10017

Printed in the United States of America

Library of Congress Cataloging in Publication Data
Holmes, Urban Tigner, 1930–   The priest in community.
"A Crossroad book."
1. Pastoral theology—Addresses, essays, lectures.
2. Priests—Addresses, essays, lectures. I. Title.
BV4011.H584   253   78-17645   ISBN 0-8164-0400-3

FOR
the people of God
who are the School of Theology,
Sewanee, Tennessee:
the students, staff, and faculty
and particularly their families

Contents

Preface

THE inspiration for this book, as well as the nucleus of the material, is the result of the invitation to give the Franklin S. Hickman lectures at Duke Divinity School, Durham, North Carolina, in the fall of 1977. I am very grateful to Dean Thomas Langford for the opportunity to share these ideas with the Methodist clergy of the North Carolina Conference, as well as with the faculty and students at Duke.

I did further work on the study for the clergy conference of the Episcopal Diocese of Hawaii, which Bishop Edmond Browning asked me to lead. I also presented these ideas at the continuing education seminar of the Montreal Institute for Ministry in January of 1978. The executive director of the institute, Dr. Art Van Seters, was a most gracious host on that occasion.

Theology should be a collaborative enterprise and this book is no exception. My friend and colleague, the Rev. Craig Anderson, worked closely with me

throughout the several drafts. His insights are re-
flected in almost every page. Georgia Joyner has been
a diligent and courageous editor; but, even more, she
has been an enthusiastic supporter. Earnest Louise
Lumpkins, my secretary, is one whom I delight in
thanking. Long hours with typewriter, scissors, and
mending tape have been necessary for the many
revisions.

A number of people have been kind enough to read
and to criticize pieces of the manuscript. Loren Mead,
Ruth Tiffany Barnhouse, Charles Foreman, Harry
Pritchett, Flower Ross, Peter Thomas, Gene Ruyle,
and others have been a part of the dialogue that produced this study. It was also part of a course I taught in
the fall of 1977. The interest of my students was a
source of encouragement amid some pretty murky
waters.

Initially I began this work with the assurance that
my friend and only editor at Seabury Press, Bob Gil-
day, would lead me once more through the intricacies
of publication. That was not to be; but I do want to
express a word of deep gratitude to him for all he has
meant to me in my writing career. I miss him.

Above all I want to give thanks for my most reliable
proofreader and most patient friend of twenty-seven
years, Jane.

URBAN T. HOLMES

Feast of George Herbert, 1978

The Priest in Community

Introduction

THE purpose of the introduction is to outline the methodology of this study. But first I need to make explicit to whom the book is written, since the title may be deceiving.

The "priest" in this study is the pastor, parson, preacher, minister, as well as priest, of any Christian congregation. The thesis is that there is in every religious community a smaller group, usually a "group" of one person, who is the priest, the symbol of the bridge between God and man to that community. Priests do not exist in isolation. Like the "quark" in nuclear physics, there is no such thing except in relationship to another thing, the community. Yet the priest is not the same thing as the community.

So the book is intended for all priests, whatever they call themselves, and to everyone who is a member of a religious community and, consequently, is party to the making of a priest. It is also my hope that those who do not consider themselves members of religious communities may find this study a way of understanding what the priesthood is about and be able to ignore the caricatures that abound in our culture. The intended readership is, therefore, much broader than the title might suggest at first glance.

It would follow that, if I intend such a wide audience, that I would be better off *not* beginning with certain sweeping assumptions about the role of the priest in the church. Often books on the subject are written from the perspective of a given school within a particular theological tradition. An example would be the discussion of the episcopacy in *The Apostolic Ministry,* a series of essays edited by K. E. Kirk and published in 1946. The method it employs is deductive. I prefer an inductive approach, attempting to identify the experience of the priest and then seeking to illumine that experience in the light of human tradition.

This means that I see myself as "revisionist" in the approach to fundamental theology as David Tracy described in his recent book *Blessed Rage for Order.* As Tracy points out, a theology should from the revisionist viewpoint discern the meaning of both our experience and the tradition and relate them in a meaningful synthesis and, one hopes, a true manner. This position involves a distinct focus on the tradition alone or a paradoxical opposition of the tradition and the world, on the one hand, and an exclusive emphasis on this world or a belief in the "death of God," on the other hand. I am speaking, of course, of questions of *method,* not necessarily to theological *content.*

But let the reader not be misled. My own outlook is conservative, in the generic sense of that word. I am convinced that we need to conserve the truth of which humankind has become aware throughout its evolution and symbolized in everything from the encoding of its genes through its symbols and myths to its philosophical systems and back again. My profound respect for the archaic, even to its outermost boundaries, guides this entire study.

This means that I am not willing to settle for an exploration of the explicitly Christian or even Judeo-Christian texts in the analysis of the tradition. These texts are central to committed Christians, of whom I count myself one; but they need to be set within the flow of the emerging symbolization of humankind's total experience of God. The few thousand years of the Judeo-Christian tradition itself comprises a relatively brief, culturally confined expression of that experience. Even if we accept Jesus, the Christ, as the normative symbol of the meaning of God for us, it is still true that too narrow a frame for understanding religious phenomena will distort the picture of their meaning for all humanity. For Americans Christianity has existed principally in the medium of an excessively masculine, univocal, northern European culture. To limit our concept of priesthood to that culture leads only to an impasse especially obvious when the question of ordaining women to the priesthood is considered in the light of past Christian texts.

This does not imply any lack of respect for those revisionist theologians who confine their exploration of the text to scripture and the Christian tradition. The Venice statement of the Anglican/Roman Catholic International Commission, promulgated in 1977, is clearly an example of such an approach and it is an outstanding document. It is obvious to me, however, that if I had confined my own exploration to so limited

a field I would not have been able to perceive the
radical nature of the priest in community.

This book certainly is often autobiographical, since I
am a priest. The most immediate source of data is my
own experience and what I make of it. For better or
worse, revealing myself, perhaps appearing somewhat
"stuck on myself," is part of the risk I take. I would
point out that this is a model of the vulnerability that I
think lies at the heart of effective priesthood. Maybe
there is something to be learned in that. The major
problem that an autobiographical approach to contemporary experience does create is a certain narrowness of interpretation, despite all best intentions. I am
a life-long Episcopalian and see the role of the priest
through the filters peculiar to that tradition. Readers
may need to make allowances and adjustments according to their own traditions.

With the revival of an evangelical Christianity today, there is a wide awareness of the tradition of Christian theology which gives heavy emphasis to a dualistic cosmology, a sharp division between nature and
supernature, and finds it very easy to confront humanity's sinful condition with the gospel. The nature of the
methodology I am following is such that some may
feel that the gospel is muted and that sin is ignored. If
what I have written in this book invites any criticism
for the lack of confrontation, I plead *nolo contendere.*
Because everything that I stand for rebels against such
a dualistic interpretation of the cosmos, I cannot engage in that easy a confrontation.

The evangelical position readily slips into a reduction of the priesthood because it ignores some of the
truths which I hold in this book, such as the historicity
of all religious texts and the centrality of the symbolic

to Christian meaning against a univocal interpretation of the Bible. Evangelicals are very fond of speaking of the "plain truth" of the scriptures. I think they fail to understand that truth comes to light only after *interpretation* of text or experience and *the perception of its meaning at many levels;* therefore, it is necessarily ambiguous. There is truth, just as there is gospel; but the former is no more "plain" than the latter is "simple."

Personally, I think any appeal to religious commitment based upon personal feelings, as evangelicals often make, is very dangerous. In the course of this book I shall explain why repeatedly. The technical name for such an appeal is called *fideism,* and it is a heresy condemned by the First Vatican Council. While I am not altogether in favor of everything decreed by that council—e.g., the infallibility of the Pope—I find they had good reasons for considering fideism heretical. Claims to the experience of God need to be subject to all the tests of human thought, culminating in reason. I have tried to follow that belief throughout this study.

It is common among those who separate nature and supernature, as well as the profane and sacred, to claim two kinds of knowing: secular and divine. My approach makes no such distinctions. The pursuit of truth by a mind illumined by God's grace is a single thing, and functions no matter what the name of the discipline under which it is arguing.

The single-minded pursuit of truth, however, is not to be interpreted to mean that I am a rationalist in the sense that truth is only available to formal operations or logical thought. I do not believe that symbolic meaning is "defective" or the easy substitute for the hard work of logical thought. Certainly the symbol leads to the thought, to quote Paul Ricoeur. But, inevitably, the effect of a univocal reduction of meaning is a narrowing of the grasp of the experience. The finite nature of the human mind demands that with precision we surrender comprehensiveness. The more comprehensive we are the less precise we will be. There always has to be a compromise at some point between the powerful multivocality of symbolic meaning and clear univocality of signative meaning.

There is no reason to apologize for using several of the human sciences as well as philosophy in building the image of the Christian priest. At the same time, it is my wish that my conclusions not be based upon a doctrinaire commitment to this or that school of thought. There are, for example, numerous references to analytical psychology, but this book is not "Jungian" anymore than Jung himself, who thanked God he was not a "Jungian." I have an admiration, however, for Jung's insights. Some will also note an interest in anthropology. I am privileged to count as mentor and friend Victor Turner, a distinguished Anglo-American anthropological theorist, but I feel no compulsion to agree with him at every point. My own philosophical training is largely from the transcendental Thomism of Bernard Lonergan and Karl Rahner, but they provide an approach, not a straitjacket.

In all candor, I hope in this book to be making one more contribution to a new pastoral theology, which is desperately needed in the church today. A number of disciplines reveal a remarkable convergence at this time in the history of Christian thought, and I want to be one of those who can point to that convergence in a way that is helpful to the church as a whole and its priests in particular. If this new approach is leading where I think it is, we will witness a dramatic shift in the direction of pastoral theology from that of the last fifty years. While it is needed, the nature of that shift can be difficult to grasp.

It is a shift to the centrality of theology for Christian action. In other words, we need to move away from a purely clinical understanding of ministry to a symbolic and conceptual understanding of the relation between God and man, and to be able to construct out of that understanding what we are to do as a Christian community. This means that the church is first of all a community for theological reflection. That is, it is the task of the people of God to seek a meaningful synthesis of the tradition and the world so our lives are illumined in a *new* way by God's vision for his creation. We can then act accordingly.

This is not easy for those unused to theological thinking. No author is insensitive to what others say of his writing, and I am well aware that my more speculative material is not read as easily as the descriptive passages. Yet it is in the speculative material that we find the ability to generalize about ministry as a whole and the priesthood in particular. The generalizations must form the core of any pastoral theology, if we are not to be victimized by the particulars of a given pastoral situation.

We have not done a very good job of teaching such a pastoral theology in our seminaries. The discipline has thankfully grown away from "my life and hard times at St. Swithin's," but in many instances has not gotten much beyond the psycho-theological model of Seward Hiltner coupled with verbatims from Clinical Pastoral Education. I do not think we can expect the priesthood to be taken seriously in a world where the social system gives it little or no real meaning until we can generalize its meaning in a clear, articulated theory.

My understanding of the priest in community is that he is an agent for the illumination of the consciousness of the community he serves at all levels of meaning. I would hope the reader in walking with me through these pages would, maybe at the end, be better able to say this is what a priest is in a way that applied to the inner city, the suburbs, or the small town, be he Roman Catholic, Methodist, or Baptist.

- ONE -

The Landscape of Reality

LITTLE things persist in our memories and nag at our presuppositions. It is such a little thing that has become for me a hook upon which I hang the subject of this study.

It was in 1957, I believe, and I had preached a sermon at Louisiana State University in Baton Rouge, where I was chaplain, on the nature of the priesthood. A priest, I had explained, was like anyone else, a human being, who lived out his life just like every man. It is wrong, I said, to expect anything more of him than we do of ourselves. Why ask for his prayers, for example, when we can pray just as well for ourselves? My server that day was Graham Schüker, a young white graduate student from South Africa. As we came back into the sacristy after the service he looked me in the eye and said, "Father, about that sermon, you'll never be just like every man to me. You're a priest, and that's different."

I wrote Graham off that day as incurably romantic.

But somehow his comment stuck with me. I am
grateful. For it has provided a slight clue to the mys-
terious experience of priesthood—and from time to
time saved me from complete perplexity. It is the experience of a power in myself as priest which is clearly
not the result of my personal characteristics, or skill, or
education, or anything else that I achieve or control. It
is the observation of a power in other priests, which
can be obscured by the perversity of human kind, but
never obliterated. It is the subject of this book:
priestly power, the ability of the designated priest by
virtue of that selection to evoke a sense of the numinous.

Graham Greene in *The Power and the Glory* tells
the story of the "whiskey priest," fleeing before the
Mexican militia, the "Red Shirts," whose task, as part
of the suppression of the church, was to eliminate the
clergy. The "whiskey priest" is a broken man, given to
all the common sins of fallible persons. He represents
a church hierarchy which has raped the people. Yet
neither he nor the people can deny the power of his
calling. Still a coward to the end, he dies a martyr for
Christ because he cannot deny his priesthood. The
power and the glory of God shine through the life and
death of this very ordinary human being with a fondness for alcohol and women.

I think it was in that spirit that I was taken to task by
my server, Graham, for a less than sensitive sermon.
People who understand the place of the priest in
human experience—and their number is relatively
small—do not consider them different because they
are morally pure or infallible. Perceptive people of
God, in my judgment, do not fall into the Donatist
heresy, believing that the power of the priest is di-

rectly related to his moral rectitude. Neither do people who correctly understand the priesthood drift into the romanticism of cotton-candy religion.

Cotton-candy religion is sweet and sticky; the American brand of it turns God into a kindly grandfather. Some of us are perhaps old enough to remember movies like *Going My Way* and *A Man Called Peter.* God in such movies suffers from an acute case of the "quaints." God's Irish or Scottish brogue is appropriately avuncular. He is utterly inoffensive, unsullied by spit, shit, and semen. An image of the same order of Jesus occurs in the movie version of *The Man Born To Be King,* in which they shaved the armpits of the actor who played our Lord. One could hardly imagine such a dehumanized Jesus threatening the Pharisees. But in fairness to the victims of nineteenth-century romanticism, let us remember that they inherited that emasculated image honestly. A long line of earlier centuries insisted on projecting it.

I contend that priestly power has nothing to do with such puritan excesses, nor does it require that the priest be one without a first-hand knowledge of sin. At the same time I am arguing that he is different, and people have the right to expect that he acknowledge the difference and embrace a unique vocation of compassion and clarity of mind that requires a disciplined moral life.

The experience I point to has nothing to do with theology or ecclesiastical polity. I would prefer that you not read what I have to say as the peculiar bias of an Episcopalian. Those Christian traditions which reject the term "priest" still inevitably designate some religious practitioners to be stewards of the symbols of the tradition. Most reasons for avoiding the term "priest" have to do with its history in Christianity. It is identified with the abuses of the late Middle Ages; it looms large in the shift from the cultic to evangelical understanding of worship. To some people the office invalidates the priesthood of all believers and of every baptized person's immediate access to God. Luther said all baptized people are priests, only some are ministers. To my mind this is not true. The individual's access to God is always in some sense mediated; and all Christians are ministers, but only some individuals are priests.

Religious practitioners, whether we call them pastor, preacher, parson, minister, convenor, or priest, I believe become symbols in and of themselves. I will contend in this study that the power of the priest functions in all religious communities, no matter what the particular functionary is called. Even when there is no such leader it chooses *explicitly*, someone is always designated *implicitly* to fulfill the necessary function of the priest.

I argue "from below." My data begins with anthropology, biology, the history of religions, and analytical psychology. I think the priestly function is natural to human religious communities. All religion has community, creed, and cult. I would add that all religion also possesses a focal person, who upholds the symbols and becomes himself a symbol to the community. But I want to make it clear that his function cannot be captured in a job description. We are speaking of something far more subtle than this. Therefore, I am in that theological "camp" that thinks grace is essential, but believes it perfects nature rather than destroys it. I also hold that nature, properly understood, renders us open to grace.

The word "priest" is derived from the Greek and

Latin for "elder," *presbuteros* and *presbyter*. *Presbyter* denotes perhaps the oldest ecclesiastical office in the church, thought by some to be derived from the synagogue. The English word "priest" in Christian theology has come to mean the officiant at the cult, which is in some sense sacrificial. My use of the word here is much broader than such a narrow definition. It is a more anthropological than a theological use. The function I describe is better captured in the term *pontifex*. This comes from the Latin meaning "a builder of a bridge," a "bridge between humankind and the numinous or God." Unfortunately, *pontifex* or "pontiff," the English word, connotes a hierarchy, which threatens to obscure my point irredeemably; so we shall stick with the term priest.

To lay a groundwork for understanding this priestly power, we need to look behind the concept of priesthood to map man's religious consciousness. This map will not show the content of consciousness, but the configuration of man's awareness within which the content lies. I speak more of the how than the what. When a neurophysiologist maps the human brain, and identifies each part of it, he is not telling us what images or thoughts the brain contains. He is telling us what differentiations that particular part of the brain can make out of that content. In a similar way I want to explore as systematically as I can the country of religious consciousness. For it is there we may find the origins of priestly power.

THE NATURE OF RELIGION

I had been invited to speak at a "prayer breakfast" at the military base where one of our seminary graduates was stationed as a chaplain. I was seated next to a

high-ranking officer, who I surmised was there because he was not high-ranking enough. He commented to me very early in the proceedings, "You know,
Doctor, I'm not 'religious,' but I do believe in the 'man
upstairs.'"

Such protestations of un-religion, with bashful
avowals of piety, can be very puzzling, unless we are
aware that people mean different things by the word
"religious." Religion, I suspect, has at least three
definitions. My breakfast companion meant, I gather,
that he did not participate in the discipline of a religious community. That is one possible meaning of the
word "religious." A second alternative, which he did
affirm, is *belief* in an ultimate source or ground of being. We may debate the validity of belief in God apart
from participation, but theoretically it is a possibility.
A third meaning is to raise the religious question and
to seek to move from a world experienced in disorder
to a perception of order. Religion by this definition is
the *process* from chaos to cosmos.

I contend that it is the nature of man to be religious
in the sense of a process of seeking final order or cosmos. As humankind evolved and developed syntactical language, and our consciousness opened to an
awareness of the future and our impending death—the
final chaos—we asked ourselves about the justice of
this apparently meaningless end. Somehow death vio-
lated our sense of order, and very early we came to
believe in spirits that care. Neanderthal man sixty
thousand years ago buried his dead with offerings of
flowers, just as Christians decorate their altars at the
funeral rites. Perhaps this was not long after the evolution of syntactical speech made possible a unique
human consciousness of death. Surely the religious

sentiment of Neanderthal man bespeaks a universal
hope for an answer to the theodicy question that has
racked every human heart for the thousands of years
since.

THE NATURE OF REALITY

As I write this the United States is debating whether
or not we are facing a critical energy shortage. The
President has called upon Congress to pass legislation
to curtail the consumption of petroleum in the belief
that our supplies are limited and will soon be de-
pleted. I asked a friend of mine in the oil-drilling
business what he thought of this proposed legislation
and he said to me, "Let me tell you what the situation
really is. What we need is the exact opposite, less control so that we can have money to drill for the oil we
know is there." I protested, "But the President says
that it is not there to be found." My friend was not
easily intimidated. "What does the President know,"
he asked, "about the *real* situation?"

My friend's assumption is that there exists a "real
situation" to be found *out there,* by which all unreasonable men, like the President, can be called into
account. I suspect the President thinks the same way
about my friend's theories. I am suggesting to you that
no such real situation exists "out there." What my oil-
drilling friend calls real is what he has concluded
from his personal interaction with the world; and the
same thing holds true for the President and each one
of us. This is why even the most reasonable persons
can disagree. Reality, meaning, and even truth—they
function synonymously—is subjectively perceived,
unless that reality be God's. But we do not know God's

reality directly, unless the true mystic can claim a direct perception. Even that reality is inexpressible!

On the basis of this illustration I want to make four points about reality, all of which are very important to this discussion.

The first is that our reality is neither something that we discover "out there" nor is it the product of our own minds. The human brain is not a photographic plate, a *tabula rasa*, on which reality impresses itself. This is naive realism. Neither does something have to be perceived to exist. This is idealism. Reality is the product of the interaction of the subject with the objective world, and thereby transcends any kind of subject/object dichotomy. This is sometimes called critical realism, meaning it takes into account the "critique" of reason by Immanuel Kant.

My second point is that no two realities are exactly alike. Since every subject's mind is different, just as everyone has his own unique fingerprints, so must the product of one subject's interaction with the objective be different from every other subject. I used to ask myself as a small boy if, when I saw "green," it was the same green everyone else saw. Now I can answer no, because no two humans build exactly the same "models" of experience.

Third, our reality never corresponds completely to our experience. The order we make of disorder, the cosmos we make of chaos, is inevitably an incomplete representation because our minds are incomplete, finite.

Finally, whereas reality is the product of the interaction of subject and object, multiple and incomplete, the more intimately involved the subjects are with one another the more closely their reality will agree. Think of three children standing before the portrait of their father. They will each see in the portrait their own experience of the father. Although each impression will differ from the other, all will be aware of the fact that the portrait does not "do him justice." But a stranger, someone who never knew the father, coming by and looking at it would not be able to tell as well as the children whether it does him justice or not.

Religion is a way of representing the experience of God. I believe that the priest is integral to that way because of the nature of the subject: religious human-kind. The image of the priest does not function exactly the same way in any two persons, nor does it identify the priest with God in anything but a symbolic man-ner. Yet given other people of God who are open to the experience of God in our contemporary world, we can find a common agreement as to the sacramental func-tion of the religious practitioner. Somehow he repre-sents the numinous in our experience. This is rooted in the common evolution of human consciousness.

BEGINNING WITH THE ABYSS . . .

Almost at the beginning of Genesis we read, "The earth was without form and void and darkness was upon the face of the deep" (1:2). The imagery is drawn from the common pre-Hellenic mythology in the world of the levant. It was called *chaos:* dark, watery, and undifferentiated primal stuff, out of which arose the created order. For Hesiod, living in Greece in the eighth century B.C., one of the original four gods was Chaos. In fact, the other three and all subsequent deities, according to Hesiod, derive from Chaos. The word in Greek means "space." In this study the abyss is a synonym of chaos.

The history of human consciousness is the account

of the ordering movement out of chaos or the abyss. Earthbound civilization is a pinpoint of light in the midst of the darkness of chaos. When I said this in 1973, the Archbishop of Canterbury accused me of offering a strange, "erudite, American theology," but I think it is a fundamental issue for religious consciousness, including Christian theology. If we abandon the image of chaos or the abyss as surrounding us we will inevitably make idols of our representations of the experience of God. This "theology" is neither erudite nor peculiar to America. Anyone who has watched his child die as he stands by helplessly, or sat in the back wards of a mental hospital, or struggled with the fact of abject, universal poverty knows what chaos is and senses its fearful ambiguity.

We never get rid of the abyss. It is within human history. Our personal consciousness arises from the infinite, dark void of our unknowing. Chaos is the source of our creativity. If you are not aware of it, meditate on where you were before you were born and where you shall be when you die. Think of the limits of the horizon of your knowing. It is always expanding, but there is the certain intuition that there is infinitely more that you do not know that is to be known. Ask yourself from whence come your dreams, that strange association of images that is unrelated to the external world.

C. G. Jung related a dream he had in which he was passing through a dark and windswept fog. He had cupped in his hand a small lighted candle. He knew that he had to keep the candle, his conscious "ego," burning. The light was threatened on every side by the darkness, but particularly by a shadowy figure that followed him from behind—his own abyss. This is a story of mankind and of each one of us. Our consciousness—our reality, our meaning, and our truth—is made from and arises from the abyss, from chaos.

A friend of mine wrote me in the spring of 1977 after three and a half months in two Indian ashrams—a retreat or conference center—and six weeks in Mrs. Ghandi's lice-ridden jails. "I learned," she wrote, "to sit [for meditation] up to five hours, and believe me that can blow the head to smithereens and lead, perhaps, to graces for which no one may be prepared. I almost suspect it takes one to the edge of an abyss where the demonic holds sway seeming to guard the numinous." (I assume she meant by "guard" something bordering and perhaps blocking the way to the numinous.) C. G. Jung might say the same thing by suggesting that the shadow, the primitive and instinctual side of self, guards the abyss or follows us through life, threatening that pinpoint of light we call the conscious ego.

We in the contemporary western world permit ourselves an awareness of only a small piece of consciousness that is the rightful heritage of people. I suspect we do this because we are so afraid of the abyss. We are right to be afraid. I wrote to my friend out of Mrs. Ghandi's jail that I liked her *image* of Christ as fierce and fiery. She called my hand when she replied, "I wonder if you would like the Christ as fierce and fiery." It is one thing to play with ideas, she was saying, and another to be confronted with something totally beyond us.

There is no controlling chaos. In an industrial age a culture's highest values are prediction and control. The closer one comes to the edge of his abyss the less he can predict or control his world and the more those values are called into question.

Perhaps we need our minds "blown to smithereens," as my friend suggests. It may be a prerequisite to the illumination at all levels of meaning of our world and the wholeness that then ensues. This illumination is the task of the priest, as I shall suggest in the next chapter. Meanwhile, we leave the abyss . . .

. . . AND MOVING
THROUGH THE WILDERNESS . . .

Think if you will of a land bordering on a fathomless ocean, which crashes against the shore with infinite energy. The coast has no uniform character, but channels the energy of the sea sometimes by steep cliffs, sometimes by a gentle shore, and sometimes in long fiords. The countryside that lies closest to the coast is wilderness, terrifyingly empty, but filled with a marvelous quiet. It slopes upward from the sea to a distant horizon. The climb can be treacherous, but there are plateaus of sweet-smelling grass as well. As you travel from coast to coast through this country, moving from the ocean, you will find that it has its own fauna and flora. There are beautiful birds and graceful antelopes, as well as man-eating tigers and poisonous snakes— which you come upon without warning. As my friend returned from India suggests, the demonic, as well as the angelic, guards the numinous. There are water-holes shaded by tall trees, and there are also geysers of boiling, sulfurous liquid.

The air has a kind of light but eerie quality. You are torn between a lonesome terror and a delicious humor by the incongruity of this wilderness world. As you progress inland these conflicting emotions do not leave you, nor does the terrain lose its abrupt quality. Nothing fits at first. But then the landscape begins to acquire a kind of primeval order. You get a glimpse of a path leading to the west. Then you discover that you are not alone. You meet others on this same journey. They are just fellow "others," like you, with no titles or distinctive dress, of all races and nationalities. You talk to each other as you walk, sometimes sing together half out of tune, struggling to share whatever it is that brings you to this wilderness. You tell stories filled with terror and humor, tell about the ocean depths from which you have come, and then about yourself and where you hope to go. You share, inexplicably, some of the most intimate details of your life.

As you walk and talk, following an ever clearer path, you come to a great river. On the other side the wilderness appears to end. You can see cultivated fields, carefully constructed homes, villages laid out with planning; and in the far distance there is a hint of the smoke of industry. You look for a way across.

Before we leave this land between the fathomless ocean and the great river, I need to make explicit what I hope is implicit in this allegory. The allegory describes our consciousness, our reality, of which there are *two* realms. The kind I describe here is one realm of that reality. The other is the land across the river. There are various ways of describing this first realm of consciousness. In earlier writings I have called it the antistructure, a term derived from anthropology. Literature speaks of it as metaphorical language or poetry. Ethological studies describe symbolic behavior. There is continuing research which seeks to ground the two realms of consciousness in neurophysiological theory, which has given rise to equating the land of which I have just spoken as "right-brain" consciousness, referring to the right hemisphere of the brain. This notion of the split brain, first developed in the 1950s, may have some foundation. At the same time, it is probably overly simplistic. What I am offering may be described as a model of consciousness in two modes.

The point of the allegory is to suggest how the human mind, not necessarily the brain, organizes experience in two distinct manners, called here the receptive mode and the action mode. These terms— "receptive" and "action"—came from psychological research. The reader should note two things. I am *not* equating brain, which is the physical organ of thought, and mind, which is our power of consciousness. Brain and mind are not the same thing, despite what materialists claim; nor can human thought be adequately explained as the epiphenomenon or the secondary symptom of determined behavior, as the behaviorists in their various guises would have us believe. Furthermore, I am not claiming final proof for the hypothesis of bimodal consciousness. I agree with a colleague of mine that, if the theory does hold, this will be the single most important discovery of the twentieth century. Until that day of proof comes, however, the model of bimodal consciousness, which I have begun to set forth in this allegory, affords a very helpful heuristic device or aid to see new possibilities in our experience.

What I have described as the wilderness is then the receptive mode of two realms or modes of consciousness. It abuts the mystery of our unknowing, or the end of our consciousness. This mode of consciousness, as opposed to the action mode, processes experience in spatial images rather than temporal images, in concrete rather than abstract ways, in holistic or relational over against analytical or differentiated models, in nonlinear terms rather than linear, analogically and not digitally, and through intuitive thinking as opposed to rational thought. A computer is analytical, linear, digital, and rational. A liturgy, which is of the receptive mode, is holistic, nonlinear, analogical, and intuitive. Because the receptive mode adjoins the horizon of our knowing, it is less conscious than the active mode. It may also be more creative and more sensitive to suggestion.

In my allegory of the wilderness the character of consciousness takes different shapes as one moves from the fathomless ocean to the great river that divides the antistructure—the receptive mode—from the structures or the action mode.

I described the coastline of the fathomless ocean as diverse, as a succession of cliffs, gentle sand beaches, and fiords. Our minds first shape our experience without assigning any image to the energy that wells up into our consciousness. These apprehensions have been called the ciphers or the archetypes of our minds. All human beings share them. Such apprehensions are not yet clothed with content. They are the point or place of the "transformation" between the infinite word of God and a finite human consciousness.

The first representation of those modes of apprehension develop in that region closest to the abyss, inhabited by symbols and diabols or, if you prefer, angels and demons. These are fundamental representations which are ambiguous, powerful, frightening, and open. We do not make them, we discover them. They "clothe" in a very immediate fashion the raw energy—what the Christian tradition calls "the word of God"—that emerges from the abyss. Symbols and diabols are particularly related to the body, hence they are very concrete. Sexual intercourse is a clear example. Birth and death are others. They contain within them the coincidence of opposites: fight and flight, love and hate, good and evil. Such representations form the basic stuff out of which human consciousness is built and the motivations out of which we act. They are the heart of all meaning. If they create a oneness in us and our world, they are symbols; if they destroy and tear us apart, they are diabols.

For the Christian, of course, the primal symbol or sacrament—the words are synonymous here—is Jesus. He is the Christ, the primordial representation of the self and the embodiment of God's love enabling our wholeness. If Christians argue that the incarnation is an act of God and not of our making, this is thoroughly consistent with a proper understanding of symbols. Symbols are not a construct of human consciousness, but a discovery—often a surprising discovery.

The next region into which we pass, moving from the shoreline of the fathomless ocean, is characterized by the consciousness of the root metaphor. This is the faint path, leading toward the west. Human beings take their symbols and they make out of them a generalized metaphor. Such a metaphor completes the sentence: "I assume the world is (like) a . . . ." One primitive tribe which I recall described the world as the back of a giant tortoise. It is to use the same figure of speech to say that the world is a great machine, a common root metaphor among some scholars in the human sciences. The root metaphor for Christians is death and resurrection.

In the wilderness of our consciousness, as we move further west, root metaphors are elaborated either as primordial myths or seminal plots. A primordial myth is a true story about the relationship between people and the God who lies beyond the fathomless ocean, from whence we have come and to which one day we must return. The story of the birth, life, death, and resurrection of Jesus is the Christian primordial myth. We enact the myth in our rituals, we sing about it, and we tell it to one another.

A seminal plot is a less profound root metaphor elaborated into a theme which shall become part of our personal story. The characters in such plots are often animals, for reasons I shall explain later. A root metaphor for me is a bear. Bears are of a particular kind of animal to me, a kind of totem which, if I were to describe them to you, you would understand as a seminal plot to my personal story.

A friend of mine, who shares the bear totem, has a continuing relationship with a bear—he calls him "Bear"—such as the relationship Elwood Dowd had with the rabbit Harvey in the play of the same name. This bear, however, takes on such reality for him that its metaphorical function is diminished. His continuing conversations with "Bear" are the seminal plot for an unfolding story that is a source of wisdom for him.

Personal stories belong to that region of the wilderness nearest the great river that divides the antistructure from the structure, the receptive mode of knowing from the action mode. They are called formation stories, because they constitute our personal script and define in an imaginative way the manner in which we "form" for ourselves the energy from God, clothed in symbol and diabol, root metaphor, and myth and seminal plot. They shape our actions in subtle ways we usually do not recognize.

I have described the landscape of one mode of human consciousness. As I have related this allegory to others various parallels have been suggested. A priest who teaches Old Testament at the Vancouver School of Theology suggests that the Bible itself, beginning with creation and ending with the heavenly city of Revelation, is the story of this journey from east to west. Another scholar, a student of Jung, believes that it is a way of seeing the process of individuation, a form of self-realization which results from our *listening* to the unconscious.

So far, however, we have come only half the way. There are three points that need to be introduced now and developed later. First, our contemporary western technological culture either denies altogether or at least drastically downgrades the receptive mode of human consciousness. We suffer from a collective extroversion. There has been an underground rebellion against such suppression all along, which is in places now coming to surface. The counter-culture of five to ten years ago is an example. But our conceptual models still avoid it. Second, the receptive mode of consciousness insists on operating with all its possibilities and risks, whether or not we choose to acknowledge it. If ignored, it is only suppressed. It will surface. Third, the roots of the priestly function lie squarely within the wilderness of the antistructure.

. . . WE COME TO THE CITY

When we cross the great river, we still tell our stories for a while. It is really the power of those stories that carries us over. There is much possibility in them and we want to do something with them. But the country is different west of the river. There are roads and fences, and villages and stores. There is the comfort of the familiar and the predictable. The terror and the raucous humor seem to be gone. There is a gentle sureness to life which provides the security for innovation and accomplishment.

Our feelings are now more tranquil. Somehow it is more important to understand what we are experiencing, so we ask ourselves: What does it mean? As we talk to others it is necessary to be as clear and unemotional as possible, in order that we may grasp our world and be in command of it. We notice that everything about us is now ordered and that the expectations that others have of us are spelled out. Ambiguity is gone, the risk of the unpredictable has vanished, and we sense the assurance of the certain.

As we move further and further from the fathomless ocean, the wilderness, and the great river, we have a clearer sense of our place and our role in a society of law, not of organisms. We find that we are entering the suburbs of a great city. As we move deeper into this metropolis, we see that its existence depends on all its inhabitants working smoothly together in a shared system. Without control and predictability of such a system this wonderful order, which is able to accomplish so much, would collapse into chaos. There is a deep satisfaction in clarity of univocal speech and precise expectations. We know what we are to do and how it is to be done. In fact, it is hard to recall the excitement of the land between the fathomless ocean and the great river, since it is so satisfying to be a part of something that works well. If the smog generated by the genius of our industry blinds and chokes, we hardly notice it, because we have forgotten how clear the air was near the ocean.

My allegory has become less and less subtle, because we all know more about the land west of the great river, the land of structures. When we cross the river we step into the country of consciousness which contemporary western culture values most highly. It is the action mode of human bimodal reality, as opposed to the receptive mode. The configuration of our consciousness moves quickly from the world of story to concept and then to system.

Unlike the wilderness, where symbols and diabols fed our metaphors and grew into myth and story, concepts and systems require precise representation of experience. It is a world designed for "professionals." The sign, rather than the symbol, dominates. There is no question about the one thing a sign represents. It is ideal data for a computer. There is no ambiguity about what is expected of us. In a society of laws, which the city must be, signs are extremely important. The only problem is that they lack passion. They are boring. They cannot inspire a great love, the building of a cathedral, or a journey around the world on a raft. Nobody dies for a sign.

Our culture is obsessed with a structured consciousness of the action mode. Our emphasis upon having and doing, rather than being, is a clear indication of the point. We may "tip our hat" to being, but I doubt that most of us could get paid much for just being. A culture whose highest values are control and predictability in the interest of production and consumption inevitably tends to compress all experience into the

univocal mold of the logical concept. We are disbeliev-
ing before anything else.

A friend of mine, a priest in a nearby parish, has
shared with me this anecdote, which to him illustrates
the contemporary disbelief.

He received a telephone call from one of his
parishioners, asking him to come right over to his
house. The caller said his aunt Elizabeth was "acting
crazy." My friend drove over to the house and found a
woman sitting in a ditch in front of the house, her arms
clasped around a fireplug. He sat down beside her and
asked her what was happening. She responded by telling a story of being all but swallowed up in chaos. She
had had to leave her home in which she had lived for
years. Nothing fit together in her new house; the
appliances did not work; even the clock had stopped.
Her nephew and his wife were harassing her and her
world was caving in.

The priest sat and listened, occasionally waving at
the traffic. Then he noticed a hedge on the other side of
the yard. Lined up behind the hedge, peeking over
the top, were said nephew, his wife, and their two
neighbors. The thought struck him—over there was
poor contemporary man, tied to the banalities of
routine, structured existence, only able to gaze with
fear into the crazy freedom of Elizabeth's antistructural world, in which only the fireplug kept her from
being swept away into chaos.

My friend is an imaginative priest, intuitive enough
to be able to enter Elizabeth's world. But such priests
are all too rare. Our overt understanding of the priest
is, again and again, framed in the form of concept and
system. Any other way of understanding priesthood is

suppressed. Consequently, someone can state as I did earlier that a priest "is just an ordinary man" and not even recognize the affront to the very notion of priesthood.

BIMODAL REALITY

I have drawn this map of human consciousness in order to try to place within man's religious awareness the function of the priest. But it must be seen as a map, not as a time line or itinerary. The truth is that the movement from the fathomless ocean, across the great river, and into the city is not a linear movement at all. It is a circular movement like walking inside of a cylinder. If we find ourselves deep enough within the city we will discover anew the chaos of the structures, and once again we will be on the shores of the fathomless ocean.

In the whole or healthy person all elements of consciousness are not only present but operative. One example of such a person was St. Teresa of Avila, who in the sixteenth century was able both to reform her religious order and to share the most illuminating mystical experiences.

Teilhard de Chardin, the twentieth-century scientist-theologian, believed that in the evolutionary process the created order has moved to an ever deeper self-awareness. Since the emergence of humankind three million or so years ago this process has taken a quantum leap toward intellectual maturity. To Teilhard, however, there is an ongoing resonance between earlier biological forms and later developments, which accords with what I suggest. There is no withdrawal from a part of the landscape of consciousness as we proceed further to the west. The mind of the human being occupies the entire country. Evolution remembers.

It appears that both in the growth of the individual and in the development of humankind, the receptive mode of thinking emerges first. A young child thinks first associatively, imaginatively, not in concepts. The action mode is not differentiated until age six or seven. Julian Jaynes, a Princeton psychologist, has argued that the differentiation and dominance of the action mode of knowing has only emerged in humankind since about 1000 B.C., and that prior to that the receptive mode, with its associative style and religious awareness, dominated. I am not attempting to revive the so-called biogenetic law that the experience of the individual reflects the experience of the race, but I am suggesting that there is a process of coming-to-wholeness-of-consciousness, both in the individual and in human beings as a whole, which does not rightly slough off what went before. Mature humanity has the capability of knowing in two modes.

Seventy-five years ago it was widely accepted anthropological theory that primitive people "thought" otherwise than civilized people. We spoke of the "primitive mystique." Primitive people "knew" in symbols and stories and civilized people "knew" in concepts and systems. That no longer holds. If we can learn anything from primitive people it is the need to reactivate the receptive mode of knowing.

A student-colleague of mine is looking into children's stories as religious education. He is particularly interested in the zoomorphic—human qualities represented in animal forms—nature of the stories and their illustrations. He has in mind *Winnie the Pooh, The*

Wind in the Willows, and the Peter Rabbit stories, as well as the cinematic cartoons of Walt Disney. I believe these stories do bear some relationship to the receptive mode of representing experience and the primordial consciousness, and therefore provide access to religious education at a deep level.

When C. S. Lewis came to believe in God between getting on and off a bus, as he told in his autobiography *Surprised by Joy,* he was on his way to the zoo! He makes nothing of his destination, but it is a tantalizing suggestion.

Recently I saw in fairly rapid succession three collections of primitive art: artifacts from the tomb of King Tutankhamen and, in British Columbia, memorial poles and shamans' masks. The zoomorphic nature of this art seemed to have the same power as the talking animals found in children's illustrations. The possibility appeals to me that both of these expressions of the receptive mode of man's knowing are rooted in the hunting-and-gathering culture that is our common and long ancestry.

It is not the size of the human brain alone that makes our species unique, it is its configuration. Within certain limits of brain size it is the brain's peculiar configuration, if the theory of bimodal thought is confirmed, which provides for a differentiation of function that gives us our creative, bimodal power of consciousness. Yet the result is a war going on inside the head of everyone of us between the receptive and action modes. The two modes of processing information are suspicious of one another. One tries to win over the other. The great tragedy of our culture is that we have settled for peace at any price and have suppressed the receptive to allow the other, the action mode, to become the normative means of representing our experience in concept and system. We do this at our peril.

A psychologist I know gave me an example of this. He was making a silent retreat at Gethsemane, Kentucky, at the Cistercian monastery where the holy Thomas Merton had stayed for years. One afternoon he found himself overwhelmed by a sense of profound joy and deeply frightened at the same time—classic characteristics of transcendental (or antistructural) experience. He had entered the receptive mode of processing experience. But this was followed by an overweening analytic period, where he became extremely critical of everything around him. In the chapel he was appalled by the seeming casual attitude of the monks in choir. They should *look* more "holy." He listened to the words of the liturgy and wondered how any sane man could believe that mumbo-jumbo. Reality was all conflict; the action mode of processing experience had seized him and was fighting the receptive. Wisely, he did not run at that moment. But the next morning he found himself in a state of mental exhaustion. Not knowing what had happened to him, he picked up and left to return to a reality more peaceful, but far more banal, where he would not always find it necessary to strive for the synthesis of the receptive and action modes.

SUMMARY

Bimodal consciousness is hypothesis concerning humankind's construction of its world or its reality. The theory does not arise from any one field of inquiry. For example, it does not depend upon verification in brain research, even though there might be a correlation between the right and left hemispheres of the brain to the receptive and the action modes of thought, respectively. Such a univocal dependency would infer that brain and mind are synonymous, which I do not believe is true. Rather, the hypothesis of bimodal awareness is a heuristic model, built from psychology, anthropology, literature, and ethology, as well as neurophysiology.

As a heuristic model, bimodal consciousness has a power of discovery and explanation of great value. In this sense it is not unlike, say, the "black hole" hypothesis in astronomy. This heuristic value is particularly true concerning the priesthood, for which other explanations appear to miss the mark in the light of our experience.

The purpose of this study is not to wrap the priest in a carefully cultivated cloud of mystification, but to try to account for the data. In the renewed interest in symbol and myth, even among those scholars uncommitted to faith in a transcendent reality, the priesthood needs to find its place. It could be that the God the priest serves does not exist, but the priest still has an observable function within the white darkness of the numinous experience, populated with its symbols and diabols, root metaphors, myths and seminal plots and stories.

It is my conviction, of course, that the priest does serve both the community and the God who speaks from across the fathomless ocean to our consciousness. The priest stands with one foot in the receptive mode and one in the action mode, a liminal or "threshold" figure, called to symbolize what he on his own cannot even imagine: that inner word of God, providing humankind with the light to see God's intention for creation.

- TWO -

Genes, Memes and Mind

THE symbolic nature of the priest is a specific image within the configuration of consciousness or the landscape of reality. As a specific symbol, it is a picture-in-itself, with certain characteristics and affect. In the first chapter we spoke of the levels of meaning within bimodal reality, with special attention to the receptive mode. We said that the priest is a symbol located in the receptive mode of consciousness, as well as a role image in the action mode. In this chapter I wish to explore the possible source of the specific image of the priest in human history with special reference to the receptive mode.

Some years ago I spent a summer working in an alcoholism treatment center. It was a kind of holding operation, in which we were doing the best we could with pretty hopeless conditions. One method of treatment in which I was trained is called Rational Emotive Therapy, the seeds of which are in Alfred Adler and perhaps best known through Albert Ellis. We tried first to get the patient to identify the "wrong thinking" which provoked the feelings that led to his drinking; then we could demonstrate how "irrational" that thinking was. Then, having done this, we could supposedly help him find new ways of thinking, which would not lead to destructive behavior. Obviously, the theory assumes that we attach meaning to experience and that all behavior proceeds from that meaning.

One question that arises, however, is: Where does the "thinking" or meaning we attach to the experience come from? I was working that summer with a group of alcoholics, some of whom had been to this treatment center over twenty times! I was pressing one of these patients to tell us why he persisted in thoughts in the face of certain experience that led him to drink. He did not take easily to my approach. Finally in exasperation he said to me, "My God, preacher, don't you know it's in the genes!"

It is popular these days to attribute certain behavior to the genes, particularly that which society sees as "deviant." The evidence is mixed, but psychotic behavior, homosexuality, and IQ, as well as alcoholism, have all been related to our genetic makeup. Sociobiology, which made the front cover of *Time* magazine (August 1, 1977), as well as a special feature that same summer on educational television, argues cogently that much of what humankind does is determined by genetic code. This includes religious behavior.

Traditionally in the history or sociology of religion such religious behavior includes three components: community, cult, and creed. The meaning of community points to a life together based upon a common experience of the transcendent. Cult is ritual or, in the Christian meaning, liturgy. The creed is what the

community states it believes, either in mythic or in
theological terms. The cult enacts the creed and the
creed interprets the cult, and participation in both
constitutes the community.

Perhaps the origins of the three components of
human religious behavior are analogous to human
language, which paleoanthropologists, sociobiologists,
and linguists say is genetically programmed. All language has nouns and verbs, a fact which may result
from the distinctive human brain, traceable as unique
for over three million years. It is even possible that the
human brain was developed for syntactical speech
through genetic change before the human larynx
evolved sufficiently for humans to utter anything but
the most basic sounds. It seems likely that humankind
makes sense of its experience in a particular way—
with a subject and predicate—because of its peculiar
genetic evolution. It follows from this that what humanity makes of its experience is necessarily limited
by its genetic structure.

Religion is the movement from chaos to cosmos. It is
a kind of language, an act of making sense of our experience to the point of attributing its ultimate meaning
to a divine mind, which analogically is like ours. God
speaks in subject and predicate. Whereas religion is
not universal to all people in exactly the same sense
that language is, it comes close. If community, cult,
and creed are not fully developed everywhere religion
exists in some inchoate form, they are certainly
significantly common cross-culturally.

A well-known practice among anthropologists is to
call in question the universality of any human characteristic by what is called the "anecdotal veto." For
example, if sexual roles are reversed in some remote

tribe, or the Oedipal complex is not somewhere evident, or a given group has no period in psychosexual
development called adolescence, anthropologists will
sometimes disclaim these characteristics as part of
human "nature," on the grounds that one exception
rules out universality. Overdoing the anecdotal veto is
called "bongo-bongoism," since to others such a simple interpretation of universality is superficial. The
persistence of community, cult, and creed in many different cultures is sufficient to make us beware of
bongo-bongoism. Perhaps we can even attribute
community, creed, and cult to the divine mind.

All this leads to a question: Is it possible that the
priest is a fourth, almost universal component to religion, just as subject and predicate are to language? It
is true the religious practitioner is absent in the structures of some societies, just as he is not present in the
action mode of knowing for some individuals. But is it
not possible that this occasional absence may only
obscure for us the common roots for all humankind of
the priestly image in the receptive mode, expressed
explicitly in most religious communities, as well as
implicitly in a few that disavow the religious practitioner? There is generally an individual or group of
individuals within any religious community, fewer in
number than the total membership of the community,
who have a leadership function rooted in the receptive
mode of consciousness. While this is obvious in the
Roman Catholic church, for example, it is equally true,
implicitly, in the Society of Friends, who expressly
reject an ordained ministry.

I have lived in two towns in which I have been
peripherally involved with a Quaker congregation. In
both instances these devoted people, whose theology

abrogates sacraments and clergy, have formed their
life around a powerful person to the point that the
congregation itself is identified by the name of that
person. "A rose by any other name"—or no name—
"would smell as sweet."

There are good reasons, on the one hand, for dis-
owning the priestly office, for it has been fulfilled in
scandalous ways from time to time. But there has always been a tendency, on the other hand, to see the
priest as of divine origin just as we have seen the
community, cult, and creed of religion as of divine
origin. This is especially the case in the priest-king
from the ancient world. Yet the modern argument in
the Preface to the Ordinal—the services for the ordination of bishops, priests, and deacons—of the 1928 Book
of Common Prayer of the Episcopal Church is not all
that different from the Egyptian belief that the
pharaoh is a son of God. It argues that three offices are
of divine origin. It seems not out of the realm of possibility to attribute this later tendency to deify the priest
to the long evolutionary history of the priestly image
and its close proximity to the abyss within the consciousness of man. This would imply that the priest is
something more than a professional in the action mode
of consciousness, that is, an agent of illumination at
many levels.

THE PRIEST IN HUMAN EVOLUTION

The history of human evolution is a widely debated
subject. There are those who believe that we can trace
a hominid development back at least five million
years, with the emergence of a hunting-and-gathering
culture of at least three million years in age.

(Hunting-and-gathering refers to a pre-agricultural society, in which food was either found where it grew
wild or game killed without any domestication of animals.) This would mean that for more than ninety-nine
per cent of our human history we have lived as no-
madic hunters and gatherers, in bands maybe of no
more than twenty-five people living by streams or
lakes. The city as a structured society of permanent
dwellings became a possibility only with the development of agriculture and the domestication of animals
ten thousand years ago. Despite some disagreement,
there seems little doubt that humankind has lived out
the vast majority of its history in or very close to the
antistructure, where it was not in control of its life
except in the most immediate sense and where the
receptive mode of processing experience dominated.

This assumption constitutes the background for
Julian Jaynes's theory that humanity prior to about
1000 B.C. was not conscious at all. Consciousness
for Jaynes is the ability to understand the world
metaphorically and describe, by virtue of the metaphor, how things we perceive function. Consciousness
in Jaynes's sense—not mine—is a function limited to
the action mode, which he attributes univocally to the
left hemisphere of the brain. Prior to the evolution of
Jaynes's consciousness, humankind in its hunting-
and-gathering state, as well as in its agricultural condition, acted in response to voices it heard in the receptive mode or right hemisphere of the brain, which it
attributed to the gods. People were a species of automa-
ton.

Jaynes further says that human beings have moved
forever into the action mode or left brain dominance
and have lost once and for all the ability to hear the

voice of the gods. I am not so sure, and I suspect this
says more about the state of Jaynes's spiritual life than
about humanity. I believe humankind is as religious
as it ever was, even if the environmental possibilities
for the expression of its religion are confused. Not only
is religion today a form of the same struggle to control
the uncontrollable, but it lies at the heart of the same
quest for cosmos that has always motivated humanity's
greatest discoveries. Whenever we suppress the receptive mode, it insists on breaking through the action
mode, sometimes in a very disruptive manner. Examples are eighteenth-century rationalism followed in
the nineteenth by romanticism, or Hegel followed by
Kierkegaard. We still hear the intuitive "voices of the
gods" in spite of ourselves.

The attempts of scholars over the last century to understand the origin of religion itself have amounted
only to intuitive guesses. We are trying to do the impossible, namely, get inside the receptive mode of
the consciousness of ancient humankind. In the
nineteenth century Edward Tylor, an early anthropologist from Scotland, thought that religious
awareness grew out of the presence of deceased persons in the dreams of the living and in the observation
of the expiration of the breath in the act of dying. Both
phenomena gave rise to the notion of the soul and then
to spirits within the objective reality, called animism.
Contemporary with Tylor was the theory that the origin of religious awareness lay in the surprise of external nature: the violent and the unaccountable in fire,
wind, rivers, and the sun. Emile Durkheim, a pioneer
French sociologist, claimed otherwise at the turn of the
century, saying that religion arose from attributing
personality to the moral power of society and from the

need to legitimize that morality. A fourth contemporary explanation would be that religion is a form of cultural reinforcement of a biological value, such as the incest taboo, arising out of our need consciously to channel behavior at a point where we can no longer depend on instinct.

While the human scientists hop among the various theories about the origin of religious awareness, they generally agree that the core of it lies in fear and wonder. These feelings arise before the mystery of life, its beginning and end, its natural environment, and its social patterns. Such fear and wonder are not a possibility until a person can acquire the sense of anticipation made possible through the evolution of language. While the animals, including pre-religious humankind, passively accepted what life brought, the advent of symbolization allowed mankind to transcend the environment in religious awareness. We can trace the rise of such an awareness perhaps as far back as five hundred thousand years ago. Two tiny bits of evidence pique our curiosity.

From 1929 to 1941 the skeletal fragments of *homo erectus,* the immediate ancestor of *homo sapiens,* were uncovered near Peking. What intrigues us is the fact that the place in the skulls where the backbone enters had been enlarged carefully with some kind of tool, so that the brains could be extracted without damaging the skulls. Presumably the brains were removed for eating; but if the sole purpose was to satisfy hunger, it could have been more easily done by crushing the skulls of the victims. We can therefore assume the practice involved some kind of ritual for which it was important to keep the skulls intact. Furthermore, we also observe that in contemporary cannibalism, where it is culturally normative, there is always a ritual purpose.

This discovery near Peking is reminiscent of the persistent cult of skulls among hominids. It is found among Neanderthal man, a subspecies of *homo sapiens*. It was practiced by the inhabitants of the oldest city of which we know, Jericho. It survived until the nineteenth century in Tibet. Sometimes the skull of particular veneration was that of the shaman. This calls to my mind a Greek monk on the island of Patmos, who showed me with great awe the skull of the ninth-century founder of his monastery, visible through a peep-hole in his tomb. Perhaps the skull, the location of the mind (although not always thought to be so among primitive people), was identified with the spirit of the ancestor. There are those who believe ancestor worship was the first form of religion.

There has also been discovered, this time on the French Riviera, the campsite of a band of *homo erectus* about four hundred thousand years old. In these remarkable remains we find that these people regularly used fire and that they probably slept around it. The remnants of their meals are found back from the firepits, indicating that they kept the ground close to the fire clear for sitting and lying down. We suspect that fire itself constitutes one of the early and primordial symbols of the numinous for man, as in the theory that religious awareness arises from external natural surprise. It seems logical to raise the question: How soon after humankind found fire did they start attributing the source of the fire itself to some transcendent reality? It is worth remembering that the fire cult was very important to those hunting-and-gathering cultures of central and northern Asia that produced the prototypical shaman. Such a shaman had among his powers the mastery of fire.

It certainly should not surprise us, therefore, to find ample evidence of ritual in the ice-age caves of both Neanderthal man, who survived until thirty-five thousand years ago, and his near contemporary and our ancestor *homo sapiens sapiens.* For example, in the remote reaches of a cave in southern France it is still possible to see heel prints of youth in the clay floor, apparently relics of a prehistoric dance. A good surmise would be that such a dance in so inaccessible a place might be part of a rite of passage from childhood to adulthood. Certainly this would match Durkheim's theory about the origin of religion.

No suggestion of the religious practitioner himself appears in the records of ancient man as we now have them until twenty to thirty thousand years ago. Among the cave paintings by Cro-Magnon man in southern France there are two enigmatic figures, one more primitive than the other, which could be the depictions of shaman-like religious practitioners in zoomorphic garb. One is a bird-man, found on the wall at the bottom of a natural shaft at Lascaux. The other is a figure dressed as a deer, found in the subterranean chamber of Trois Fréres at the end of a narrow forty-yard passage.

One needs to be very cautious about reading too much into such paintings. Anthropology is right in hesitating to conclude from present primitive culture the nature of humanity's prehistoric past. We know of present cultures that have no explicit, designated religious practitioner. Yet it is difficult to imagine any kind of religious tradition which does not have certain persons charged with carrying on the tribal lore and ritual.

It could be a group of elders, the old women of the tribe, or just somebody who arises·spontaneously and naturally. What evidence we have indicates that when someone is designated in some manner it might take the form of the shaman-like figure of the hunting-and-gathering cultures.

With the rise of agriculture ten thousand years ago and the evolution of a more focused religious consciousness, we find in numerous localities the worship in some form of the Great Mother. The Great Mother, often called the Queen of Heaven, is the generic term for the feminine deity, common to those early societies dependent for life itself upon the fertility of the soil— and of the women. She has many names in various cultures—Asherath, Isis, Aphrodite, Demeter to name a few—but has a common root in human consciousness today. No matter what her name, she possesses a personality defined in the myth that surrounds her cult. In the scanty remains of early agricultural communities we find countless little clay figures of pregnant women, apparently some kind of votive offerings for fertility. These suggest a ritual connected with the Great Mother and possibly a priesthood, arising from the shaman-like predecessors of hunting-and-gathering cultures.

Probably the early agricultural communities were theocracies, in which the ruler was a priest. By the dawn of history this is a well-established practice. In early Egyptian civilization the pharoah was a divine being, identified with the myths and rituals related to the fertility cycle. It is also true of the Sumerian culture, with its infinite number of deities. Such a priestly role, coupled with a theory of divine origin, gave a unique sanction to the power of the ruler.

The tendency as time passed was for the role of the priest to be separated from that of the king, as happened later in Egypt. Such a process paralleled the growing dualism in religious cosmology. As long as we identify the arena of divine action with the tribe and its environment the congruence of the sacred and the profane naturally follows. As we divide the arena of divine action from the natural world to a supernatural world (e.g. heaven) then the priesthood that serves the divine action is separated out from the rulers of the natural world, the kings. By the time we come to the roots of our own Greco-Roman culture this process has taken place, which may explain why western humanity has inherited a dualistic cosmos, divided between the sky God and the earth.

The emergence of a dual authority in culture accentuated the priest as located in the action mode. He served the masculine sky God, the Great Father, who stands above the society, judging and legitimizing its life. This is the supernatural God. Yet it is possible that such a priest is still a part of an evolving stream which flows from its source where a primordial figure stands, rooted in nature—the Great Mother.

THE PRIEST IN RACIAL MEMORY

In the case of the alcoholic who attributed his behavior to his genes, we see an example of the debate between the influence of heredity and environment. My alcoholic patient was saying that his disease was largely genotypical, while my therapy was based on a phenotypical presumption as to its cause. The term "genotype" refers to the genetic constituent of an organism, such as a human being, and "phenotype" to the results of the interaction between the genotype and its environment.

In suggesting generally that the image of the priest evolved over a long period, and in saying particularly that the shaman-like image in primitive and archaic humankind feeds the understanding of the historic priest (rabbi, shaikh, minister, presbyter), I raise the question of whether the symbol of the priest is genotypical or phenotypical. How would one explain the possibility that the later twentieth-century cleric evokes a memory in the religious community of the shaman-like figure on the walls of the caves in southern France? Is it in our genes? Or is it culturally transmitted? Is the content of the priestly image purely theological and abstract, or sociological and professional, or anthropological and primordial?

Behavior that is rooted in the genotype is usually described as instinctual. The human infant comes into the world with a sucking-and-clutching instinct. It is likely this is rooted in our pre-hominid past. Language is instinctual. It is virtually impossible to keep a child from learning to speak. I am not sure that the religious drive is not instinctual: humanity's instinctual need to make cosmos out of its chaos. Perhaps even the expression of religion—community, creed, and cult—is somehow rooted in its genes. After all, humankind is by instinct a social animal; its ritual behavior can be found in other creatures as a form of communication; and its need to name what it experiences (the beginning of creed) is a part of language. The issue now is whether the religious-practitioner-as-symbol is instinctual in humanity or not.

The long history of such a figure, as we traced it in the previous section, may imply much or little. If the

shaman-like personage within prehistoric humanity
has a history as long as humankind has been hunting
and gathering—three million years, perhaps—or only
as short as the span of Neanderthal and Cro-Magnon
man—fifty to eighty thousand years—is it still possible
that this numinous image is carried in the human
genotype, an imprint left by countless centuries of
practice?

The Lamarckian belief that humanity, along with all
other organisms, assimilates into its genetic structure
environmental characteristics which are then passed
on to its offspring has been discredited in favor of
Mendelian genetics. Building upon the earlier
theories of Darwin, it maintains that the environment
has no active influence on the information carried in
the genes; instead, evolution proceeds by spontaneous
genetic mutation and natural selection of those mu-
tants favorable to survival. These are still open questions, however, for which geneticists have no sure
answers.

There are certain disjunctures in organic evolution
which are hard to explain by a simple cause and effect,
even with allowance for sudden spontaneous leaps.
The development of the genotype is perhaps related to
the environment. Experiments in lower organic forms
have from time to time raised some interesting questions, if they have offered no solutions.

In 1962 initial experiments with a common flat-
worm, the planaria, caused considerable stir in the
scientific world because the experiments seemed to
indicate that learning could be chemically transferred
from one animal to another. A group of planaria was
trained to respond to light, then ground up and fed to a
group of planaria not so trained. According to the first

experiments the second group, after eating the first group, also responded to the light the way the first group had been trained to do. Repeated experiments, however, have yielded different results.

Generally the experiments have little value for us, but they do highlight an area of research in neurophysiology. This is the attempt to discover the engram or memory molecule, the chemical basis for memory in the brain. If such a permanent, tangible chemical trace is identifiable, it could simply be unique to the individual brain—but what if it could interact with the DNA, the chemical structure of the gene, in such a way that this "memory" was passed on from generation to generation? There is evidence that long-term memory does change the protein structure of the gene.

Some recent experiments with amoebae have indicated that the molecular structure of that creature can be altered by the environment and carried on after subsequent cell division. Of course, in these simple organisms, which multiply by cellular fission, subsequent cells contain much of the protoplasm of parent microbes. This is not true of the offspring of mammals. We know of no parallel phenomenon in the higher order of animals.

Therefore, to reflect on the possibility of the *active* impact of the environment to shape the genotype is not only to push to the edge of genetic and evolutionary research, it is probably to pass over into the realm of science-fiction. A much better case can be made for a *passive* channeling of the developing genotype.

This is what is known as the theory of genetic assimilation. If we go on the theory that there are millions of possibilities for the encoding of the genes, the question arises why a certain pattern evolves. The answer might lie in the relation of the genotype to the environment, which not only produces the phenotype, but also the particular genotype itself. For example, why is there a certain "collusion" at a point in history of physiological changes in humanity (opposing thumb, relation of the skull to the backbone, true bipedalism, and changes in the configuration of the brain) which come together to produce *homo sapiens sapiens*—i.e., you and me? One theory that provides an answer is genetic assimilation. In this theory the environment "selects" among the almost infinite encoded options present in the genes, producing a genotype which has the highest likelihood of survival. Skin pigmentation—black, shades of brown, red, yellow, and white—is an obvious, if not very radical, illustration of genetic assimilation. Through this process of genetic assimilation the genotype is passively shaped by the phenotype.

It appears that we are speaking of the genes as the basic unit of organic life, and in fact sociobiologists do claim this. They go so far as to say that primary human behavior is really the way genes fight for survival. As one author describes them, the genes are "selfish." They control our behavior, and the genes make sure much different from us. The genotype has a stability due to the replication ability of the DNA. This could include the memory, that store of images from which humankind draws to give meaning to its experience.

The stability of an organism depends upon its ability to replicate, to produce the same genotype repeatedly. We sometimes overemphasize spontaneous mutation in evolutionary theory, forgetting that it is most important that the DNA, the building block of the genetic molecule, reproduces itself over and over again. This is why hominids three million years ago do not look

much different from us. The genotype has a stability due
to the replication ability of the DNA. This could include the memory, that store of images from which
humankind draws to give meaning to its experience.

Ethologists and sociobiologists go on to say, however, that what makes humanity unique is its ability to
interpret experience and to build a world of meaning,
which is called *culture*. This culture provides a parallel replication of information which is characteristic
of the phenotype. Humanity does not live just by instinct; more than any other animal, it lives by cultural
meaning. In fact, the genes of humankind have produced culture as a new way of handling their needs.

One ethologist, Richard Dawkins, has coined the
notion of the "meme" (rhymes with "cream") which is
to culture what the gene is to the gene pool. Whereas
the gene leaps from body to body by means of sperm
and ovum, the meme leaps from brain to brain by
means of imitation. Where instinct can no longer suc-
cessfully contribute to humanity's survival, culture
takes over. The memes embedded within culture are
what we call tradition, running from customs of dress
to, perhaps, the incest taboo. There is no suggestion by
Dawkins that the meme is related to a supposed engram transmitted by biological inheritance.

Religion is a form of culture. Tradition repossesses
enduring memes. As I pointed out earlier in this chapter, ethologists and sociobiologists, taking their cue
from Durkheim, say that, while society produces culture, religion gives culture a sacrality which imparts a
compelling motivation and stability to its precepts. It
makes for a social order which protects humankind
from chaos. Religion endures not because it is true but
because, according to the sociobiologists, it renders

the arbitrary structures of the social system necessary. It enables society to replicate itself with a vengeance.

In Durkheim's system, particularly as expressed in its ethological adaption, the priest is an action mode servant of the *status quo*. His task is to reinforce the memes of the tradition, whose purpose is to guarantee the stability of the social order. The enemy of the priest is chaos. My argument, since I believe the priest is initially rooted in the receptive mode, is very different from this. This is because there is more to reality than univocal relationships of genes and memes to behavior. The data of humanity's experience, including the process by which sociobiologists come to their theories, protests against any reduction of the information coded within the genes and memes to mere signs. There are symbols in every memetic configuration which point beyond the culture, and similar symbols may well be found in genes which lead us beyond the brain. The brain and the mind are not synonymous.

If this were a book in fundamental theology in general, we would have to pursue this line. Since it is a foundational exploration of the symbol of the priest, we rather need to ask ourselves again where in humanity's memory we locate the source of the priestly image. I have suggested as possible answers humanity's biological evolution and cultural tradition: the genotype or the phenotype or both. A much easier case can be made for the phenotype, but I am not sure this adequately explains the consistency, the cross-cultural commonality, or the strength of the symbol. Perhaps it lies in both the genotype and the phenotype.

Yet there may be a third alternative. C. G. Jung believed early in his career that the objective psyche or collective unconscious with its archetypical images—which would include the priest—was inherited and was a common dimension of the human gene pool. He always believed that objective psyche extended beyond the various phenotypical expressions of different cultures. Later in life he implied something quite different: a sequence which begins with God, moves to the collective unconscious, and finally is realized in the individual consciousness. Humankind is not only genotypical and phenotypical, in this view, but also "nootypical" (from the Greek word for "mind," *noos*), foreshadowing or imaging the *mind* of God. It is to the relative independence of mind from brain that we can attribute human freedom and humankind's ability to transcend biological or sociological destiny, while yet limited by both.

Sir Alister Hardy, a noted Oxford zoologist, notes in his Gifford lectures of 1963–65 that there is a problem in explaining evolution either through classical Mendelian genetic theory or by means of the modifications of genetic assimilation. There is a missing factor in evolutionary theory, Hardy says. The secular world-view would perhaps find his solution to the problem of the missing factor untenable. It has certain appeal, however, if one grants the possible existence of God. For Hardy suggests that there is a cosmic mind, which through mental telepathy guides the process of evolution. It is a provocative notion, not at all far from the speculations of Teilhard de Chardin, the Jesuit paleoanthropologist.

In Hardy's theory the racial memory of humankind is not merely a matter of our genes or our memes, but is *more* than biology or sociology. It is also made in the image of God's mind, and humanity's memory participates in God's mind and his purpose. Such participation would date from the time in our primordial past when our ancestors asked the purpose of life and sought to form an answer.

THE PRIEST AS HERO

If Jung, Hardy, and those others who question the final adequacy of genetic and/or memetic theory are right, suddenly the function of the priestly symbol takes on a richness that has great appeal. It is more congruent with human experience.

For what is unique to humankind is not just our biological development or our social systems, but the structures of our meaning, that is, our intentional consciousness. A chimpanzee can be taught to recognize itself in a mirror, employ simple tools, and parrot a few words. It cannot, however, contemplate its own death at some future date or write a poem. An occasional overzealous ethologist misses this point; but on the whole there is wide consensus that this ability to question experience is unique to man.

In the evolution of human consciousness there is a movement from a naive participation in the world, where everything is seen as a projection of oneself or where every self is seen as part of a great whole, to an ever increasing awareness of the boundaries between the self and the inner and outer environment. The movement is to a sense of being "over against," and further to the point of an identification of the self with the rational mind. This process is traced by numerous students of human thought from various points of view. Such an evolution of consciousness is not the unique claim of one school of thought or even allied schools of thought.

What does this mean for the evolution of religious consciousness? We cannot say with any certainty what the common religious character of prehistoric culture was. There are those who have argued that religion began with a belief in a high or sky god, but if it has any correspondence to fact, it has no relation to later monotheism. Others point to totemism as typical of very early religion, but this cannot be proven either, any more than a number of other possibilities. Probably there is no one common character to prehistoric religion beyond an inchoate feeling that there is someone behind nature that influences humanity for good or bad. The first religious ritual may have been as simple and yet as profound as the thankful acceptance of food as the gift of divine being. There is no reason for thinking ritual started out as magic, the attempt to control the source of our benefits.

The cave paintings of Cro-Magnon man, which are relatively recent in the history of humankind, imply a belief that by a form of sympathetic magic the spirit of the deer or some other game could be evoked to provide a successful hunt. Judging from modern discoveries of the carefully preserved skulls of the great cave bear, Neanderthal man felt it necessary to propitiate the spirit of the bear he killed for food and warm clothing. There is an immediate sense of the spirit that lies within every object of one's experience, and there is a belief that our spirits can be one with all other spirits.

The shaman-like religious practitioner was, perhaps, one who had the most immediate commerce with the spirits. It is possible that originally all humans felt an equal immediacy, although I personally am doubtful of this. Certainly there came a time when persons, perhaps because either they felt possessed or because their father passed on to them the rituals, or both, served the community as a bridge to the spirits.

As a bridge the religious practitioner is a source of understanding even more than knowledge or information. The point of this distinction is that understanding involves relationship with what is the object of knowing, whereas knowledge is information about the object. The priest initiates a movement in his people to a greater understanding of their experience. This is what is meant by naming the priest the archetypical *hero*. The chaos that threatens all human life, but of which primitive man is probably as a rule more aware than we, is given a semblance of order by the actions and person of the shaman-like figure. Life, with its birth and death, plenty and famine, health and disease, is related to some power that transcends it and suggests a kind of consistency, even a glimmer of purpose.

Side by side with the cave paintings of Cro-Magnon man can be found figurines, some crude and others quite beautiful, depicting the naked female form. Sometimes the woman appears pregnant. The so-called "Venus of Laussel," a bas-relief carving found in a rock shelter in southern France, is a striking case in point. She has exaggerated breasts and hips, as many of the figures do. The sculpture may be thirty thousand years old. Across Europe and into Asia countless carvings of the feminine symbol are being found, dating from the same era. There is a particularly striking little figurine of a very fat woman that was found in Austria. Another one, which the noted mythologist Joseph Campbell calls "Our Lady of the Mammoths," was discovered north of the Black Sea, placed within a circle of mammoth skulls. We are dealing with peoples undoubtedly dependent for life itself upon the successful hunt of that great prehistoric beast, and somehow these images form a part of their quest or thanksgiving for a continuing fecundity of life.

Campbell believes that the nature religion identified with the mystery of woman and the sympathetic magic of the Cro-Magnon cave paintings bespeak two different religious patterns. He then suggests that shaman-like persons would be expected in the latter, but are not characteristic of the former. This may be true, but some bearer of the tribal lore would seem to be logically necessary in nature religion, as I have already argued. Story is as old as language, I am sure, and someone has to be the storyteller.

The nature religion of prehistoric man seemed to develop into a fairly well articulated cosmology by the time of the rise of agriculture. The mystical connection between the fertility of the soil and the creative force of woman is one of the basic intuitions of what is called "the agricultural mentality." It marked the movement of humanity's consciousness from a more diffuse, uncontrollable sense of the spirits on the edge of the abyss to a more focused symbolism within humanity's structures of meaning. The priest as hero may well have led this movement.

One of the earliest cities of which we know (eight thousand years old), Catal Hüyük in modern Turkey, was filled with numerous shrines in which abound the figures of the feminine symbol, now more clearly a goddess. In the focused nature religion of Catal Hüyük and similar cities stretching from Turkey to India, as well as among peoples around the world, the Great

Mother, known in her local forms by many names, is
arising to consciousness.

With the emergence of the worship of the Great
Mother humanity comes to a further awareness of its
world. The experience of death and regeneration, as it
informs life itself with all its promise and horror, is
caught up in the symbol of the nourishing and devouring feminine symbol. Julian Jaynes accuses paleoanthropologists of going too far in seeing all feminine
artifacts from this period as fertility symbols since, he
argues, there was no need for such a concern in a naturally fertile world. I disagree. No matter how fertile
the land might appear to be, no one could be sure what
it would be like for the next year's crop. Humankind
was dominated by the receptive mode and saw nature
as basically fickle. The god of nature, the Great
Mother, is usually considered capricious.

The role of the priest in all this is hard to identify.
There are few records from eight thousand years ago.
The priests of the Great Mother probably appear most
clearly in the much more recent grisly fertility rites of
the Aztecs of Central America. One can, however, also
extrapolate a picture of the priests from such shrines
as that of Anath, the Canaanite Great Mother and the
sister of Baal who revels in the blood of human sac-
rifices, and Ashtaroth, whose temple is literally built
on the skulls of infants. We can be only horrified by
such practitioners of religion unless we think of the
overwhelming fear of chaos with which they believed
themselves threatened; we then understand their need
for order. Three or four thousand years ago an individual life was not very precious, since there was little
sense of the individual self over against the community, and life itself was short.

Whether as the shaman-like figure of the cave rituals or the priest attending the Great Mother, the function of the religious practitioner was *to make life bearable,* if not fruitful, in the face of humanity's consciousness of the precarious, chaotic nature of life. This function reached a culmination as the priest became the person who freed humanity's consciousness from slavery to the Great Mother and her capricious behavior. As the television advertisement of the mid-1970s said, probably unaware of invoking primordial symbols, "It's not nice to fool Mother Nature!"

The priest who by his message of understanding effects this liberation from the feminine symbol is even more the hero. Prototypically he is the "slayer of the dragon"—a root metaphor embodied for Christianity in the fictional St. George or St. Michael (Revelation 12:7). Prior to the Christian myth we find the same theme in the Old Testament, where Yahweh conquers the Leviathan in the great deep (Job 41:11–34) and when Zeus, the head of the Greek pantheon, kills Typhon, the child of Gaea, who is Mother Earth. The same story is also found in Egyptian, Hittite, Sumerian, and Canaanite religion. The serpent or dragon is the symbol of the Great Mother from prehistoric times until this very moment. Look, if you will, at the feet of the Virgin standing on the serpent in St. Catherine Laboure's vision of the Immaculate Conception. In the Old Testament in its early forms, with its abhorrence of fertility cults and its attribution of temptation to a serpent (Genesis 3:1–5), there is the account of a series of heroes culminating in Moses, who led the people from the Great Mother into a new consciousness of God as the sky king.

This is the priest who brings the people across the

great river into the action mode. In the Old Testament
the symbol of God *par excellence* is the Torah, the
univocal law. The priest at his best is the prophet,
who recalls people from the ambiguity of the receptive mode, with its temptation to bask in the feminine
symbol, to the law and its call to justice. He is the sage
of the wisdom literature, sharing the practical understanding of the reflective man. Such a priest over and
over again slays the dragon, the Great Mother, like
Elijah on Mount Carmel (1 Kings 18:20–40—remember that Baal is the brother of Anath).

This development in religious awareness is an expression of the basic growth in human consciousness.
Jaynes identifies it as the time of humankind becoming actually conscious. I prefer to think of it as the
time, first, of the individuation of the ego from the
collective, and second, the growing identification of
the distinctive self with the rational mind. It is, of
course, the rise to preeminence of the masculine symbol and the subjugation of the feminine symbol and its
embodiment, woman. A distinct dualism is created.
The "father" is separated from the "mother" by a
great gulf. There follows a tendency to identify evil
with nature, mother, and the feminine. Into such a
world of meaning Christianity came, and then later
Islam. There is no wonder that a fundamental
puritanism, born of a rational reduction of human consciousness, pervades Judaism, Christianity, and Islam.

The hero is the one who brings light. The Hellenis-
tic world at the time of Christ saw light as reason (in
Greek, *logos*). The high priest is the Logos of God, the
Christ, the light of the world. To understand is, very
quickly, to have a rational grasp of one's life under the
sky God, the masculine God of reason. The Great

Mother and her principle of eros, unifying and devouring love, returns to the subterranean reaches of the unconscious. The priest as hero becomes a servant of reason and its less rigorous ally, common sense. We will return to this subject in the last chapter.

FOLK RELIGION

As human consciousness evolved further into the action mode it had to repudiate the receptive mode. The masculine heroes of the universal religions— Judaism, Christianity, Zoroastrianism, and Islam— slew the dragon. They "conquered" the darkness of the Great Mother, the tomb/womb, the abyss, or hell. They also created an illusion: that we are free of the Great Mother, and that nature religion or paganism is no longer a part of humanity's reality.

This illusion has led us to "theologize" as if true humanity were *only* the nootype, detached from the genotype and phenotype. When some theologians rejoiced in the 1960s at the realization of "religionless Christianity" and the victory of secularism, they apparently believed that humankind was no longer led by the spirits. Some of the leaders in the feminist movement, who declared women's freedom from "anatomical destiny," really thought that the genotype has no power over the nootype. Similar thinking has led us to define the priesthood in purely rational terms, describing it as a profession, a role within the structures of the social system.

But nature religion, with its spirits, lives in contemporary humanity as much as it did in the past. We call it folk religion. We have not grown beyond the receptive mode with its peculiar religious phenomena.

Michael Pye, an English lecturer in religious studies, defines folk religion as incidental religious behavior, unrelated to religious grouping. Folk religion for him includes the occult, nature mysticism, astrology, divination, ghosts, and perhaps a more than scientific curiosity about parapsychology. Pye's definition is superficial—as indicated by his use of the word "incidental"—because it lacks the kind of undergirding conceptual basis that bimodal consciousness gives us. It is better to say that folk religion is the name we give to religious meaning and behavior which refuses to be suppressed by a religious system of the action mode of consciousness. For three thousand years the action mode has sought a dominance over human religious awareness, and achieved a particular victory in the sixteenth century. Its success, however, has only resulted in a "possession" by the receptive mode rather than an effective use of the antistructure. The tragedy of the witch trials at Salem, Massachusetts, in the late seventeenth century is an example of such possession.

A happier illustration of the semiconscious persistence of the receptive mode comes from my ministry. Once, when I was serving a congregation in North Carolina, I visited a successful farmer and a pillar of the local Evangelical and Reformed Church (now part of the United Church of Christ). The conversation with him turned to the farmer's almanac, a "bible" of folk religion. I asked my friend, "What do you make of the recommendation that you should plant your peas on Good Friday?" There was a long pause during which I imagine he was pondering what he should admit to me, the representative of the established religion. "Well," he said finally, "I've seen fields of peas

planted on Good Friday standing by those planted the
week before. The Good Friday plants were six inches
higher than the others." With that he said nothing
more.

A vendor went through that same congregation
while I was there, selling "pictures of Jesus" for
seventy-nine cents. One marvelous old man, eighty-
five years old, showed me with a hush of reverence
what he had bought. It was as gaudy a picture of the
Sacred Heart as I have ever seen. The Sacred Heart is
a part of Roman Catholic folk religion and a feminine
symbol of the Christ.

One does not have to look far at all in the history of
Christianity or in our ministry to discover that folk
religion, that receptive consciousness of the experience of God, cropping up again and again, is attached to
the feminine symbol. The cult of the Blessed Virgin is
only one of the more obvious illustrations. Protestantism, which was originally motivated in part from a
renewed need to suppress folk religion, is not free
from its own expressions. The feminization of Jesus in
Protestant art is a case in point. Judaism, the father of
masculine religion, has the *kabala* and the eastern
European Hassid, who recovered a certain feminine
element in their religion.

The Grubb Institute, an English agency involved in
research into the nature of human institutions, including religion, has a theory about religious behavior.
They believe that humanity is religious by nature and
that this nature expresses its religion in an expanding
series of concentric rings. At the center is animism
(meaning, perhaps, the attribution of a diffuse spiritual
cause to life's events), followed by the faith of the
hero, then folk religion (i.e., nature religion), and fi-

nally universal religion. When universal religion collapses, we fall back on folk religion; and when there is
no folk religion, the society collapses.

I think this theory is helpful, although I would be
more inclined to place the hero as the priestly catalyst
of the movement between the various rings, reducing
the number of rings to three: animism, folk or nature
religion, and universal religion. Furthermore, I would
insist on the value of a healthy two-way movement.
Each ring has its function. All of us live before God in
the abyss, in the receptive mode, and in the action
mode of thinking. It is not concerned with change, it is
movement of various modes of consciousness.

The Grubb Institute points out that folk religion is
essentially conservative. This is true of the receptive
mode of thinking. It is not concerned with change, it is
not interested in the issues of justice. The Old Testament prophets rightly railed against a fertility religion,
which was unmindful of the poor and the oppressed.
But the answer to this is not to fool ourselves into
thinking that an abandonment of folk religion is possible or even desirable. Neither is true. We need a
priesthood that builds on the strengths of both the receptive and the action modes, as well as acknowledging the abyss.

Humanity's mind is neither a blank tablet on which
the environment writes, nor a computer designed for
solving only rational problems. Somewhere deep
within, we are hunters-and-gatherers and worshippers
at the shrine of the Great Mother, as well as rational
creatures. Fly on a helicopter over any great American
city on a late Friday afternoon and witness the atavistic
journey, as thousands of urban dwellers stream out of
the city for thirty-six hours to re-create themselves by
some stream or lake in the country. They are going

"home," just as surely as the king salmon fighting their way upstream to return to nest, spawn, and die. More often than not, sad to say, we cannot quite risk the authenticity of that ancestral home, and we take with us the creature comforts of the city. We never quite make it back to our primordial origins. Our emotional and spiritual health would be better for it if we did.

An example of a more successful atavistic journey, which by its great popularity supports my argument, is the program known as Outward Bound. This program emphasizes survival in the wilderness, without any of the comforts we have come to expect in our urban living, as a context for self-discovery and the building of personal confidence. It seems to me there is no doubt that it draws us back to our primordial, human roots.

One recent summer three of my children were together at a church camp in the woods and hills of northern Alabama. They returned after ten days all excited: "We are changed! We have found ourselves and one another! We will never be the same again!" My six-foot, sixteen-year-old son sat in our living room and wept, not because he was sad but because of his joy over the discovery of a new—I would say receptive—consciousness. Is it too much to suggest that the memory of a more open, less structured life that is part of our human heritage edged into their consciousness there in the woods by the stream? The religion of church camps is often much more a folk religion than the universal religion of the ecumenical councils. Is it not possible that the receptive consciousness of that camp is the true source of caring and intimacy? I know that many a call to the priesthood is realized at that camp and others like it.

I do not wish to propose a simplistic notion of the

innocent primitive as opposed to the depraved urban dweller. One does not have to return to the cave and forest to discover the receptive mode, and much has been gained for mankind by entering the action mode and being freed for a while from the Great Mother. I am not a Luddite or follower of John Ruskin. Anti-rationalism is a disease to be feared. Yet what are they looking for—the stockbroker who climbs mountains, the corporate executive who makes furniture, or the schoolteacher who skis during vacation? I suggest it is the world of the receptive mode.

Contemporary man has been deprived of his birthright. The technological society, with its one-dimensional values of control and prediction, leaves us confused. It often works to explain away intimations of the numinous or reduce them to univocal categories, rather than risk the chaos. These atavistic yearnings lead us to the edge of the fathomless ocean. At the risk of chaos, yes—but to ignore them is to shield oneself from the awareness of God's immediate presence in our lives.

SUMMARY

I have two friends, both of whom are analytical psychologists, graduates of the Jung Institute in Zurich, and both of whom are priests. The difference in them is that one finds his priesthood utterly consistent with his commitment to much that Jung's teaching implies, while the other perceives a disjuncture between his profession as an analyst and his role as a priest. The first was raised in the Catholic tradition of Anglicanism, which sometimes reluctantly accepted folk religion, and the other comes from the heart of the evangelical tradition, which abhorred and rejected folk religion, revealing its sixteenth-century roots.

The sixteenth-century argument over the cultic versus the evangelical understanding of Christian worship missed the point about the nature of priesthood. The priest is much more than a sacrificial official. He is a mystagogue. To be a mystagogue is to lead the people into the mystery that surrounds our life. The mystagogue comes out of the darkness of man's evolutionary past, charged with the responsibility of deepening humanity's understanding of itself by word and action, by the very nature of the priest's presence. Any capable religious practitioner does that, whether he calls himself Jewish or Christian, Catholic or Protestant, Baptist or Episcopalian.

The need is for the priest to do it well. That requires that he intentionally let it happen. The priest is not called to return to the past or to recover some kind of neo-shamanism. Based on the heuristic model of bimodal consciousness and grounded in a kind of "pagan Catholicism," the priest, the effective priest, lives in the wholeness of bimodal consciousness. He is the hero of humanity's unfolding consciousness as it evolves from genotype to phenotype to nootype.

- THREE -

The Shamanistic Roots of Priesthood

I had come with my wife and two very young children to visit my sister and her family. They were living then in the Charleston, South Carolina, Naval Yard, inasmuch as her husband was stationed at the hospital there. He had proudly shown me around the place, including a trip down into a submarine and a VIP tour of a modern destroyer. The skipper of the destroyer, a lieutenant commander, had been very cordial to me.

Several days later my sister and brother-in-law invited some friends over for drinks to meet my wife and me, including the lieutenant commander and his wife. I wore my clericals at the cocktail party, being about three years into the priesthood and consequently neither knowing any better nor having the money for an additional wardrobe if I had. The lieutenant commander clearly fixed on my priesthood from the beginning. Well into the party, he cornered me in the den. "Now that I have drunk enough to have the courage to ask you," he said to me in a threatening manner, "I want to know what makes you 'tick'!"

It is altogether remarkable that this guardian of our nation's liberty had to have three drinks to find the "Dutch courage" to ask a very young and intimidated priest what makes him "tick." I did not have the slightest idea what makes a priest "tick." I have spent a considerable sum since then to find out what makes me "tick," as well as what makes the priest "tick." I doubt very much that I could explain even now to the lieutenant commander, in his categories, what I have discovered since. I have observed again and again that the priest is, by virtue of what he is, a challenge to the presuppositions of the action mode of processing experience. My argument in this chapter will be that the image of the priest is understandable only in terms of the receptive mode of knowing. It is not possible to understand what makes a priest "tick," if we are trapped in the action mode of thought.

This entrapment has contributed substantially to the identity crisis of the clergy over the last generation. There has been an unwitting acceptance, without qualification, of the categories of interpretation of the action mode cut off from the receptive mode. For example, there is the professional model of the priest, which depends, as I said at the end of the last chapter, upon a structural role definition. In a book published in 1971 I cited with some approval an unfavorable review given James Glasse's book, *Profession: Minister*. At that time I did not know Glasse, which was fine until I met him in 1974. When I was introduced to him his first comment was: "Oh yes, you're the one who didn't like my book!" Such is the price of honesty. My discomfort was short-lived, however, because Glasse went on to add that he agreed with me and that some day he hoped to write a book entitled *Beyond Professionalism*. This could be the title of this study.

The contemporary infatuation with the action mode of interpreting the priesthood is illustrated in the well-worn story of a dowager, an old "pillar" of the parish, who, upon being introduced to the new curate, aged twenty-five, asked him, "Young man, how can I possibly learn anything from you?" His rather glib reply, as the story goes, used to strike me as impertinent. I now think there is a gleam of truth in it. "Madam," he is reported to have said, "when I speak to you I am two thousand years old."

I propose here that when he speaks or is simply present-as-priest to her he is more than thirty thousand years old. He is not accountable to time. This is what makes him and every other priest "tick." This places the priest primarily within the receptive mode of knowing.

THE CONTEMPORARY MYOPIA

The problem in understanding this approach to the priest is the contemporary American mind. The problem may be attacked by assuming two sets of interacting characteristics of the contemporary mind. One such set is the rational or irrational; the other set is the sentimental or cynical. The contemporary mind does not have the categories to understand the priesthood because it tends to be either rational and cynical or irrational and sentimental. The rational and cynical mind is usually a reaction to the irrational and sentimental, and vice versa.

When I think of a rational and cynical mind my memory returns to a conversation I had in my senior year at college. I was a student in the university in which my father had taught since 1925, and I had gone to a party with my parents, attended largely by their contemporaries on the faculty. One professor, who had known me since I was a toddler, asked me, "Terry, what are you going to do when you graduate?" I told him I was planning to attend seminary. I recalled as I answered that he once had been a clergyman, and therefore I recognized the reason for the particular sadness in his voice when he replied, "Don't ever lose your faith."

Obviously I have remembered this conversation for a reason. It embodies for me the particular dilemma of my father's generation, who in the face of the attacks upon religion by biology, sociology, and psychology succumbed to the rational and cynical frame of mind. This was the only alternative they saw to the irrational and sentimental faith of nineteenth-century American piety.

The professor who spoke to me of losing his faith lost it fifty years ago at the nadir of American theology. But his cynicism, coupled with rationalism, still lives. As late as 1976 I wrote to a section chairman of the annual meeting of the southeastern branch of the American Academy of Religion, offering in response to an advertisement in the AAR journal to read a paper at a session of a meeting. The request was to discuss a subject to which I have devoted a good portion of my scholarly life. I can only surmise that my title, "The Very Reverend," created a certain anxiety in him, for he replied in a most cordial manner that he would be delighted for me to read my paper as long as it was "scholarly" and not "confessional." Obviously for this man these were two mutually exclusive categories.

They are, as well, for the irrational and sentimental mind. I spend far more time than I would prefer with romantic Christians, who believe that God speaks to our feelings and that reason is the enemy of revelation. They are symptomatic of the theological climate of America.

I recall only recently the genuine incredulity of a person who, after some public lectures, could not understand why I would expect religious belief to be reasonable. "What does reason," she said in a quiet and inquiring tone, "have to do with God?" Afterwards, sensing my frustration, my host explained that the inquirer had just come through a very traumatic experience and had found Jesus. I was not comforted. My question to him was greeted only with silence. "How does she know she has found Jesus unless somehow it appears reasonable?"

The American revivalist tradition is part of the anti-intellectualism endemic in our culture. For it the experience of God never transcends our feelings and, consequently, lacks self-criticism. Bumper stickers proclaiming that the occupant of the car has "found it" have invited ridicule running from "We never lost it" to "We lost it in some college town." The reason for the retort is that the antecedent of "it" is never defined beyond a solipsistic warm glow.

If the priestly symbol is to be understood effectively by the contemporary mind it will have to break out of the rational and cynical or irrational and sentimental alternatives. The possible solution lies in the sensible mind. The word "sensible" here means becoming cognizant or being deeply aware.

In an essay on the metaphysical poets of the early seventeenth century T. S. Eliot laments what he calls the "disassociation from sensibility" in western, particularly English, literature since the metaphysical poets. Eliot describes sensibility in terms which evoke the definition of bimodal thinking. Sensibility is the ability to devour the whole experience, with all its contradictions, and to make a new whole meaning without leaving anything out. It does not sentimentalize chaos or maintain control through cynicism. It knows that the nurturing, devouring Great Mother lurks beneath our domesticated notion of God, as well as the spirits within the abyss. The sensible person is one who enters the antistructure and risks the demons to meet the angels. The sensible person would understand the words of the German poet Holderlin, "Where danger is, there is salvation also."

Examples of the contrast between sentimentality and sensibility may help to explain the meaning of the latter. I think of Elvis Presley's funeral with its entourage of matching white Cadillacs, hysterical adolescent females aged fifteen to fifty, and reporters asking people what Elvis looked like in his casket. (Thank God for the one man who had the courage to reply, "Dead! What else?") Compare such bathos to the funeral of John Kennedy fifteen years before and you have a vivid reminder of the difference between sentimentality and sensibility.

A further contrast is to be found between sexual intercourse as entertainment or the expression of warm feelings and sexual intercourse as the sacrament of the most intimate human relationship. There is very little in our culture that counters the more casual view of sex with the sacramental understanding. Instead, the only alternative offered is a stultifying and repressive neo-Victorianism. This lack of imagination thwarts a recovery of sensibility.

A still further contrast lies between, say, the liturgy written by John Wesley and a Methodist service to which I once found myself party. I was the preacher one Sunday morning, and found my sermon followed by this litany.

> LEADER: Today the Lord steps into the air once more to taste its color and feel its song. He inhales the thoughts of children, the breath of yesterday, the fantasies of to-morrow . . . , and he wonders if his children are too old to celebrate their dreams.
>
> PEOPLE: Let us spin him our dreams.
>
> LEADER: Someday soon people will celebrate life everywhere.
>
> PEOPLE: But we would like to do it right now, wet and wild rising with our Lord.
>
> LEADER: Someday soon people will send up balloons in church.
>
> PEOPLE: Turn tired old cathedrals into cafeterias.
>
> LEADER: Paint gravestones as bright as the sun.
>
> PEOPLE: Know they are beautiful, black, red, white, yellow, men, women, boys, girls.
>
> LEADER: Become as free as the man called Jesus.
>
> PEOPLE: Play kickball with cripples in the park.
>
> LEADER: Love a person because of his or her humanity.
>
> PEOPLE: Accept a person for his or her individuality.
>
> LEADER: Laugh with the growing spring flowers.
>
> PEOPLE: Dance with the falling summer rain.
>
> LEADER: Baptize babies with love before birth.
>
> PEOPLE: Celebrate Easter as angels do.

LEADER: Hang Christmas banners from the moon.
PEOPLE: Yes, someday soon, people will start to live like that, but we plan to start right now!
LEADER: Right now, Lord.

I promise that not one word is changed from the Sunday bulletin. Would somebody tell me what it means to "baptize babies with love before birth"? If ever there were a lack of sensibility, with ideological cliches dripping with sentimentality, this is it.

It would be easy for the reader to conclude from what I have said so far that my thesis rests on a fondness for the "paleolithic revival" of the counterculture of the early 1970s. In reflecting upon man's long history of hunting and gathering, I am not suggesting a return to the river bank and the caves. This would be folly. As I have said before, this is no post-Ruskin tract. What I do believe is that we need to embrace the rational and sensible and avoid the cynical, the irrational, or sentimental. For only in this way are we going to be aware in a helpful way of the function of the priest in the consciousness of the individual and the community.

SENSIBILITY AND THE PRIEST

What happens if we move from the irrational and sentimental or the rational and cynical view of the priest to a rational and sensible grasp of the priestly image? Three concrete examples come to mind involving money, death, and sex.

Many years ago I was in a meeting of the board which managed the affairs of the university chapel of which I was chaplain. We were discussing the impending canvass of every member and our need to raise the level of giving in the congregation. The subject of motivation for raising this money came up. I commented that if you get someone to give sacrificially then you have deepened his commitment, because money is a sacrament of our lives. My treasurer's reply was, "You priests are so impractical! People give because they know we need to pay the bills."

This is a common illusion of the rational and yet cynical mind: clergy are impractical, they do not understand the business world. For while a few clergy may be naive, it is far from impractical to say that money is sacramental. I know of instances where the level of giving in a congregation has been tripled by telling people to put their money where their heart is, while at the same time attendance at service there has doubled. Psychologists tell us that money symbolizes feces, self, power, or sex. This may come as a surprise to some, but most priests are well aware of the deep personal identification people make with their purse or wallet. If clergy have a problem with money it is not ignorance as to its power, but rather an excessive fondness for it based upon years of living in marginal poverty.

It is almost trite as well to point out that, except for the followers of Elisabeth Kübler-Ross and a few burial societies, our contemporary culture treats death in a very sentimental fashion as well. No one dies, they "pass away." Some undertakers seem dedicated to promoting the illusion of immortality. Not infrequently the attempt is made to have the priest become an ally in this great coverup.

It is common to note that we hide the event of death

in hospitals and nursing homes, without any sense of
the appropriate function of the priest. On one occasion
I asked a nurse why she had not informed me of the
approach of death for a parishioner of mine. What
strikes me as I think about her response is that she
literally had no way of processing my inquiry. She was
struck dumb. "Priest" together with "deathbed" did
not compute. Finally she mumbled, "It never occured
to me. You would only have been in the way."

Of all people who should know death intimately it is
the priest. I sometimes say to my students, "Make a
point of meditating upon your own death." This is not
a morbid bit of advice. It seeks to equip us to walk
with those we serve to the very gates of death with no
illusions and yet with a certain hope. I will be eter-
nally grateful to the young mother aged thirty-two,
dying of cancer, who looked me in the eye and said,
"Now I need you. Tell me what it is to die." I had no
glib answers, but she confronted me then and still
does call me from the grave to live my vocation not as
many would suppose, but aware of the stark finality of
death.

Charles Merrill Smith's delightful book *How to Become a Bishop Without Being Religious* is for me a
study in the sensibility of the priest in the face of a
prevailing sentimentality. In a particularly funny chapter he describes the average congregation's unwilling-
ness to accept the fact that their pastor's children were
conceived in the normal fashion. He explores all the
possible options: adoption, osmosis, the cabbage patch,
and so forth. The problem of envisioning the priest as
having intercourse is the same one that underlies the
horror of having one's pastor overhear them telling a
dirty story: our sentimental view of sex.

I think it is time the truth were told. In the long history of Christian ministry the besetting sins of the clergy are always the same: alcohol and women. To women, with the advent of women priests, we may have to add "and men." I have discovered that high on the agenda of many priests at clerical gatherings is the exchange of off-color jokes. There is a healthy release in this. Where doctors are often reticent to discuss intimate details of their patients' sexual lives, no priest is worth his salt who cannot speak of the mysteries of conception and birth as well as death. But this carries a certain danger. It awakens the sleeping dragon, the Great Mother, which we only think is slain.

I do not condone the fact that clergy are vulnerable to sexual sins. We should stop pretending, however, and know why the symbol of priest carries a strong erotic element. It is worth noting that the earliest possible depiction of the religious practitioner, the bird-man in the cave at Lascaux, reveals a very obvious erect phallus. John Updike's novel *A Month of Sundays* recounting the sexual exploits of an Episcopal priest is no fiction. To be a priest is by necessity to share deeply the antistructural dimensions of people's lives, to face the erotic realities both in their demonic and angelic form, and to discern what makes whole and what destroys. The choice is to be an ineffective "cold fish" or to risk being consumed. We must choose this risk, but prayerfully in the grace of God.

THE SHAMAN

A search for a rational sensibility to the priest leads to the enigmatic figure of the shaman, of which I first spoke in the last chapter. The word itself comes from the Tungus language of the contemporary Siberian tribes. It has come to be applied to the religious practitioner common to all hunting-and-gathering cultures, past and present. A hunting-and-gathering culture is particularly aware that man is not the master of his fate and by inference understands grace and our dependence upon God.

The most prominent characteristic of the shaman is his ability to heal, but this is not all. The shaman is an archetypical figure or symbol. He is a *theotokos,* one who "bears God" to humankind. He is the specialist in the human soul. His particularly distinguishing characteristic is magical flight, an out-of-the-body experience which takes place during a trance or altered state of consciousness. It is universal to shamanism. The purpose of this flight is to converse with the spirits in order that the shaman may expand the consciousness of those he serves.

A good shaman has great power at image-making. He is an utterly convincing performer, a superb storyteller who makes present for a people their vision or myth of the world. The shaman's dress, his masks, his instruments are used with trickery and irony to turn the world of his clients upside-down, to crack their common-sense presuppositions imposed by the structures. In this sense the shaman is a personified parable, who leads us out into the antistructure to the very edge of the abyss. In fact, in the mythology of some seafaring tribes, he goes down into the fathomless ocean to talk to the spirits.

Shamans are creatively weird, not just crazy, as it used to be common to think. One researcher discovered that Apache shamans generally suffered from character disorder with hysterical and compulsive attributes, but only to the degree that they were successful actors and had a creative potential. After years of reading psychological profiles of applicants for seminary I have come to think that there may be such a thing as creative pathology. Shamans must be by their very function nonconformists, inhabitants of the antistructure and skilled in the receptive mode of processing experience.

It is noteworthy that the shaman does not subscribe to the Talmudic injunction that "cleanliness"—moral or physical—"is next to godliness." His use of chemical substances, such as peyote, jimson weed, or tobacco, is well known. Perhaps not as celebrated are the reports of prodigious sexual potency, although it is noted that the shaman is usually very discreet in fulfilling his need.

Since Shamans are characteristic of hunting-and-gathering cultures, it follows that much of their power involves the control of game. They identify with the spirit of the animals and themselves take on zoomorphic character. This is the main reason we assume the two paintings in the caves of southern France were shaman-like: their zoomorphic form. Shamans perform in the guise of deer, buffalo, or wolves. In museums in the Northwest there are vast collections of shamans' masks which illustrate the countless zoomorphic possibilities of the shaman. All of this ties in once again with the zoomorphic characteristics of the receptive mode of knowing.

It is customary in anthropology to distinguish between the shaman and the priest. The shaman is typical of tribal cultures, he gets his power directly from the spirits, he is independent and part-time, he focuses on the individual, and he uses spirit possession, trance, and frenzy. The priest is typical of structural role definition. He receives his credentials as a result of special training, he is the member of an organization and works full-time, he leads groups, and he participates in routine acts of adoration, prayer, and offering. But there have arisen those who question this distinction. The *mara'akame* of the Huichol Indians of Mexico, as well as the religious practitioner of the Campa Indians of Peru, seems to possess the attributes of both shaman and priest. Here and elsewhere there is a certain overlapping of function which contributes to the question of whether or not the shaman and priest evolved independently.

This has lead some anthropologists to suggest that the shaman as religious practitioner is the original and the generalist, of which the priest, the diviner, the prophet, and the medicine man or healer are derivative specialists. There is convincing evidence that the Hebrew prophets were skilled in bimodal thinking and firmly rooted in the shamanistic tradition. It is apparent that as a culture moves to settled habitation and agriculture, it experiences a differentiation of religious function. This is characteristic of the pueblo culture of the American Indian. By the time we come to someone like St. Paul, who described numerous differentiations of the religious practitioner (1 Cor. 12:28), thousands of years have passed since the culture moved from the culture of the shaman to the domestication of animals, to agriculture, the city, and to the rationalist reduction of humankind. Yet behind such differentiation the shaman remains deeply buried within the consciousness of man, shaped by three million years of hunting and gathering, the image of the one who mediates between the people and the spirits.

For C. G. Jung the shaman is the mana-person. Mana is an Oceanic or South Pacific term, meaning divine power as seen in its ability to effect material results. Mana is the divine energy from the fathomless ocean that beats upon the shores of our consciousness. It is this energy which is the sole evidence for the presence of God, inasmuch as we do not know God's essence.

Mana, or divine energy, is not something one who is wise can claim for his own. The magician, the demigod, or the anti-Christ might believe that he controls the mana, but the mana-person knows better. For the mana-person the power lies between the modes of consciousness, and while he is not possessed by it, neither does he possess it. The mana, of which he becomes so keenly aware in the antistructure, is a power infinitely greater than he, but a power which the effective shaman can embody and use to create and not destroy. As we become aware that nature has the final word and we are not masters of our environment the mana-person can harness the power of the antistructure to enhance our ego-potency. The good shaman is like the effective electrical engineer. He knows enough to respect the power of what he studies and to use it for good, but he cannot claim it as his own.

THE BLACK PREACHER

When we think of shamans in this country our minds usually turn to the archaic religion of the American Indian. The best-known manifestation of the shaman is the medicine man, a term derived from the French word for doctor, and bestowed by the French Jesuit missioners upon the Indian healer. As I have already indicated, the medicine man is a differentiation of the shamanistic generalist. One theory about how the medicine man heals is that he induces the client to heal himself by providing an image of order and form, which the sick person appropriates in utter faith to overcome confused and chaotic images that threaten to overwhelm him. This is, if we think about it, very much related to the definition of religion in the first chapter, and its further exploration in the second chapter. But the archaic culture of the American Indian is so different from our own, and even the medicine man so removed from our western symbolism, that it offers little help for understanding the priest's function in the contemporary culture.

This is not true of the black preacher. While the black preacher bears a superficial resemblance to white American Protestant clergy, he has retained/developed a style of his own, unsullied by the prejudices of a rationalist, patriarchial bias brought over from northern Europe by our ancestors. The source of the black preacher is the African witch doctor.

Jung says the mana-person is one who has identified the feminine symbol or archetypical image within himself, called the anima or eros. If ever there were a chronic psychological problem in northern European males, particularly the North American variety, it is our marked inability to make such an appropriation. We have suppressed nature religion. The American black, with his roots in Africa and its many matrilineal societies, has no such problems. Consequently, he is able to embody the shaman function with far greater ease and grace than the white priest.

I have a fondness for the writings of H. L. Mencken, who was probably as bigoted an iconoclast as American letters has ever known. But he had a telling way of

putting things. One of his observations has to do with
his opposition to sermons and bible study. "A solemn
high mass", he says,

> must be a thousand times as impressive, to a man with
> any genuine religious sense in him, as the most power-
> ful sermon ever roared under the big-top by a Presby-
> terian auctioneer of God. In the face of such over-
> whelming beauty it is not necessary to belabor the
> faithful with logic; they are better convinced by leav-
> ing them alone.

Mencken's point is well made, unless that "Presby-
terian auctioneer of God" is black. Because the black
preacher lacks the compulsion "to belabor the faithful
with logic"; he creates an atmosphere in which the
pressures of society are momentarily lifted, and the
people are in touch with God. With the power of his
words he can fly with the Spirit and carry us into the
antistructure. He is a master storyteller who knows
that the power of the oral tradition has always ex-
ceeded that of the written word.

Henry Mitchell, a black Episcopal priest, has described the black preacher as a "linkage figure,"
which is jargon at its worst, but well intentioned. What
he means is that the black preacher has sensibility. He
can help his people internalize the whole of their experience, with all its apparent contradictions—old
and new, familiar, and unfamiliar, traditional and
modern—and build from it a cosmic whole. He is
shaman-like, a different sort of hero from those the
early white settlers in this country brought from northern European post-sixteenth-century Christianity.

Often the black preacher is faulted for his extravagance: elegant clothes, expensive automobiles, and trips to Europe—even when his people are poor. But then we forget that we are puritans, whether our label is Roman, Anglican, or Reformed, with an obsession for logic. We do not understand the shaman to whom people brought expensive gifts when they were starving. It is as illogical as Mary Magdalene's extravagant "waste" of the precious ointment in anointing the feet of Jesus.

The ideal black preacher knows the meaning of suffering. He pays a price for the way he lives. His own image of prosperity is a symbol of hope for his people upon which they make demands. It is not necessarily an expression of spiritual pride or a surrender to the materialism of the world, although it can be.

Lest I paint too ideal a picture, the black preacher has a shadow side. He is capable of an entrepreneurial perversion of the ideal or of a misdirection of the power, such as Eugene McDaniels recounts in his song "The Reverend Mr. Lee." This song, most familiar in a rendition by Roberta Flack, tells of the fall when tempted by "Satan's daughter" of "a very big, strong, black, sexy Southern Baptist minister," who finds he does not "have it together" as he thought he did. But at his best and with no puritan ancestors, the black preacher does not confuse parsimony with humility as we do. Like any good shaman he knows that humility has its roots in the earth *humus,* in spit, shit, and semen, and has nothing to do with being stingy and mean in spirit, even if it does require risk.

The earthiness of the effective priest exemplified in the black preacher is one way of describing the sensibility of the priestly image. It is hard for us, conditioned by many centuries of thinking of the divine as a "sky God" who is the law-giver, the rational word, and the disciplinarian, to think of his being served by those who are rooted in the earth. Our religion is too masculine. If it were more feminine and the divine more an "earth God" or the Great Mother, we would be freer to understand the power of a chthonic priesthood—i.e., one serving the subterranean gods. It is the power of the earth that the black preacher can represent. Such power is full of risk, but to avoid it is to capitulate to sentimentality or cynicism.

THE PRIEST AND PROJECTION

It is a fairly common experience in the life of any priest for little children, aged four or five, to call him "God." It used to bother me, until someone told me not to waste my time assuring the child that I was not God. After all, he would learn better when he grew older.

I now believe that we never outgrow this association, we only suppress it. Some people would deny that in the priest we "see" God, but I think we do. When a parishioner comes to talk with his priest he perceives this as a conversation with God through the priest. This is because the priest as symbol evokes the expectation of the shaman in our unconscious. It is the shaman who talks with the spirit. This unconscious association is very much at the root of asking a priest to pray for you, when logic would say you could do it just as well for yourself.

Recently a priest told me he was brought up in that school of pastoral care which considered routine parish calling a waste of time because it did not "accomplish" anything. The conversation in a pastoral call goes nowhere, there is no issue on which to focus, and "after all, you only see the wife." But his parish protested, as many do, his failure to make routine parish calls. He continued to fight with them until finally a wise layman said to him, "Tom, you know why people want you to call on them? They want to get God in the house."

A specific illustration of this expectation was given me by a priest who heard me tell the admonition given Tom. He had responded to a notice of the sudden death of a parishioner and was met at the door by the very distraught wife, who cried, "Where is God?" Without any reflection at that moment, he said, for reasons he did not then understand, "God is here," obviously referring to himself. The wife's reply was of great relief, "Thank God."

Perhaps the most striking example of this identification of the priest with God was told me by a United Church of Canada clergyman from New Brunswick. He was visiting in a hospital and the nurse came to him and asked if he might come and help them with a patient who was extremely upset. They were having no success in settling her down. The clergyman was wearing clerical garb. As he entered the room the patient grabbed him around the knees and cried out to him, "God, please forgive me!" He assured her of forgiveness and she immediately became quiet. I am reminded of the story of the demon, who cried out to Jesus from a man possessed by an unclean spirit, "I know who you are—the Holy One of God" (Mark 1:24).

A good portion of my priesthood was spent in the predominantly Roman Catholic culture of southern

Louisiana. Any priest there knows the frequent experience of being asked on the street to bless a medal, a rosary, or just the person. I often wondered what was in the minds of those who asked me for a blessing. Myron Madden, a chaplain at the Baptist Hospital in New Orleans, has helped me understand this. He points out that in the act of blessing we give away our potency or energy. We impart or, better, we identify mana, divine power. What we bless becomes changed or becomes an instrument of change, because power is the ability to effect change. The request for a blessing is related to a person's desire for change, for healing, and for wholeness. The priest is perceived as one who has the power to change people.

This perception is rooted in our receptive mode of thought, which universal religion would have us abandon. It is a projection of the power within one's own reality to change, to be open to the presence of God in our particular life. But what do I mean by a projection? As I have argued throughout this study, the totality of bimodal consciousness is within us all, whether or not we are aware of it. The abyss of the fathomless ocean, the wilderness of the great river, and the concepts and systems of the city are all an intrinsic part of the mind and its configurations as we process our experience and construct reality, meaning, and truth. What the action mode, so beloved by the western mind, does not grasp is that our concepts and systems are only *representations*—and rather inadequate ones at that—of our experience. But symbols, metaphors, myths, and stories operate within us all the time. In them we represent the same experience, usually unconsciously.

The priest, by virtue of his shamanistic grounding,

"catches" the symbols and myths within our receptive mode and objectifies them for us. This is not a conscious process, but is rooted in human history from the beginning of any religious consciousness. Another way of saying the same thing is that the priest is the "hook" on which we "hang" certain symbols or archetypical images that are within us. He is the object of our projections. The priest or shaman as mana-person is the mana-person within our own inner wilderness, representing to us the presence of God within.

The light the priest sheds on the community is as the light of the moon. This is one way of describing what is said here. It underlines the fact that the priest is both different from the community and yet exists only, in one sense, by virtue of the community. What is seen in the priest is the reflection of what is the presence of God in the people. This is true for the priest in the receptive mode. In another sense, that of the action mode, the priest is as the sun. He has a light that is his own.

This objectification in the priest of what is within us is projection. It is not something unhealthy, but a normal process, common to us all, by which we become aware of our own inner life. Projection is the first stage by which we move from unconsciousness to consciousness. In projection, unconscious content within us is "projected" by our process of making sense of our world and attached to an external object such as the priest, but this projection appears to be the object's meaning. This meaning is different from the meaning of the thing-in-itself, however, and actually belongs to our inner selves.

We know the difference between the meaning of a thing-in-itself and our projected meaning upon the

thing by the emotional content in that meaning. If
something "gets under our skin," so to speak, it is
likely to be the projected meaning that evokes that
feeling. For example, people tend not to have neutral
feelings about priests. Priests readily "get under our
skin," negatively or positively. The power of the shaman to evoke our unconscious reality is there, for better or for worse. A primordial symbol or diabolic meaning, right from the edge of the abyss, is brought up,
projected, and laid on the priest. Our reaction is
affect-determined, which means that it pertains to the
receptive mode and is not "censored" by the action
mode or logical thought. God's presence within each
of us, as perhaps the devil's presence, becomes objec-
tified in the image of the priest.

The fact is illustrated in an incident to which a student of mine was witness. It involved his university
chaplain. He was with his chaplain when word came
to the priest that a man across the street had just shot
himself. The priest was asked if he would come and
help the wife, although he had never met her. Of
course he did, and very quickly he was driving with
her behind the ambulance carrying the body of her
obviously dead husband. As they drove to the hospital
the woman screamed in anger at the priest. All the
frustration of a tragedy foreseen but not prevented led
her to the edge of her personal abyss. There were the
demons; and with uncontrollable invective, she laid
them on the priest. He became the "hook" for her
inner agony. Some would say that this was inappropriate behavior. I am not so ready to make that judgment.
This is the role of the shaman, to enter into the wilderness and to fight the demons. From there, my student
tells me, healing followed, because the priest had not

run from her anger, from her abyss, but stayed there in the wilderness and shared with her the healing angels that, with the demons, inhabit that place by the fathomless ocean.

ILLUMINATION

The clue to how the priest does this lies in the shaman's use of images. He is by vocation one who raises and expands the consciousness of those he serves. He is the hero who brings the light, even if it means returning to the darkness of our atavistic religious feelings. The appropriate use of the projections of the people becomes the most powerful tool in making others aware of the reality of God that lies, often unknown, within their own world of experience. We need to keep in mind both (1) that man's conscious reality is only a pinpoint of light in a world of darkness, from which God speaks, and (2) that the task of the priest is to enable a further illumination of our consciousness from out of the darkness.

Man has a natural openness to God's word. Man looks within, as well as without, but his looking must be consistently free of stereotypical representation. St. Paul uses the image of man as a clay pot, into which the transcendent treasure is poured. The important thing is that there be no lid on this vessel. The openness easily becomes clogged with our sin, our preconceptions, and our personal agenda. We have to be turned upside-down or shocked into a willingness to entertain the new, so that we may remain open.

This openness lies at the leading edge of our knowing. If we think of God's word coming to us from the darkness of mystery, then there is a twilight of the

known, yet not quite known. It is the world of being
coming into consciousness. The priest should inhabit
this twilight world.

I agree with Max Scheler that the fundamental attribute of God is *mentality*. God is mind. I mean by this
that God is best known in word, be that word symbolic
or conceptual, which is the creation of consciousness
or mind. The priest, perceived in terms of his
shamanistic roots, serves to expand and raise consciousness. Knowing is the equivalent of being. This is
a truth which undergirds not only theology but
psychotherapy. Psychotherapy begins with insight or
consciousness of what makes one what one is, and
moves to provide an awareness of other options into
how one can live and *be* different. A priest is not a
psychotherapist in that sense. He is a mystagogue, an
instrument of God's purpose in heightening or expanding the consciousness of people and their possibility for being as he leads them into the mystery of
their own nootype.

The word used by the church Fathers for such in-
crease of consciousness is *illumination*. Justin Martyr
in the second century, for example, says that the wash-
ing of baptism is to be called the "illumination." He
and others have good New Testament precedent for
illumination. The author of Hebrews uses precisely
the same Greek term for baptism (6:4, 10:32). The
word means to lighten, as the sun lightens the world,
as well as to instruct or teach.

Illumination is something we all want. I remember
this being brought home to me in a dream. I was with a
group of people and someone came to us and said, "It
is time to go." We got into an elevator and went down
for a long time. The elevator door opened and we entered a great room, with concrete walls and floor and a

barrel ceiling. It was all covered with coal dust. Our guide said to me, "You are in hell." I saw a phone booth over on the left side of the space. I went in the booth and dialed God. This mellow, baritone voice came on the line. "This is God," it informed me. I said, "God, I just wanted to let you know that I am in hell." The voice replied, "Oh, is there anything I can do for you?" I thought and then said, "No, it is rather better than I imagined; but I could use more light." The dream continued one more step. As I got out of the booth I saw an illuminated sign which read, "Help our distressed firemen."

Of course, it was not really hell I had entered, but the depths of my own self, which I found not as bad as I had imagined them to be. Yet I needed then—and, like everyone, need now—more light so that I might enter the dark corners of my life and be whole. This light is, as Christians believe, the Christ.

The referent in Hebrews and the Fathers for the term illumination is a sacrament, a ritual in which are embedded the symbols of our Christian faith. We have the tendency to think of illumination, if we think of it at all, as the teaching of concepts and systems, moral precepts and doctrine. Illumination may well come to this in the final analysis, but it begins with the symbols, metaphors, myths, and stories of the receptive mode that enlightened our minds. The sharing of the mind that is God with humankind begins at the primordial level of our reality and only then appropriately moves toward conceptual refinement. You can have a religion without a developed theology, but not without ritual and myth. The result of illumination is the ability to reflect in a way that makes the difference between sensibility and sentimentality.

In 1968, when Martin Luther King was martyred, in

many cities across the land Christians assembled to witness, while elsewhere people gathered to loot and burn. In Memphis, where King was killed, there was a procession of thousands to the city hall. At the head of that procession was the dean of the Episcopal Cathedral, clothed in the vestments of his office, carrying the processional cross from that bastion of upper-middle-class religion. It was for us today weird behavior: a man in cassock, surplice, and cope, carrying a great jeweled cross bespeaking the wealth of its donors, walking down a city street. It was also an act of illumination.

The priest, by virtue of his shamanistic origin, is called to illumine the people. Remember our argument from the first chapter that religion is the representation of the experience of God. Furthermore, recall that the shaman calls up a world view for his people, he creates images of order to heal a sense of chaos. This illumination of cosmos is not just in what the priest does: preside at the liturgy and preach, although this says a great deal about good preaching and good liturgy. Good liturgy and good preaching evoke the receptive mode even more than the action mode. A priest illumines the people more by *who he is,* the inhabitant of both the wilderness and the city, and is equally at home in both.

SUMMARY

It is popular in some circles now to equate the priest and the shaman and suggest they are the same thing. That is more than I wish to say. The purpose of this study is to explore the nature of the ministerial priesthood in an industrial age. The shaman is the religious practitioner of a hunting-and-gathering culture, and he

can no more exist in our world than a computer pro-
grammer can function in a neolithic village. This is
why I have spoken of the shamanistic roots of the
priesthood, rather than the priest as shaman.

It is my contention that the reality that was the shaman's is still part of our reality, although to our great
loss it has been suppressed. Furthermore, since the
priest is one expression of the differentiation of the
shaman's function, there is a direct relationship between the shaman's reality and the priest's reality. The
priest exists to enable us to find the illumination of our
life that comes from the symbols, metaphors, myths,
and stories of our heritage that are the powerful media
of God's word to us. He is called to be a particularly
"sensible" person and to evoke in us this same sensibility, the bimodal process.

The challenge of the priest is, then, to learn from the
shaman, but not to imitate him. This is very important
to understand. I have discovered that previous sugges-
tions I have made that we explore the meaning of the
shaman have been misunderstood in this regard. The
intense psychological drama that is unique to the shaman, including the trance and the magical flight, are
not part of the contemporary priest's necessary skills.
To attempt to imitate them does not lead to a creative
weirdness, but leaves him a simple crazy fool. But
what the shaman illumines does belong to the priest:
the journey into the wilderness. This truth is summed
up in a moving manner in the words of an Eskimo
shaman to the Danish explorer Rasmussen:

> All true wisdom is only found far from men, out in the
> great solitude, and it can be acquired only through suf-
> fering. Privations and sufferings are the only things that
> can open a man's mind to that which is hidden from
> others.

- FOUR -

The Priest as Angel

AT one stage in the development of this book I had occasion to present my thesis to a group of clergy, among whom was a Methodist pastor who told me this anecdote. He is a chaplain in a small West Virginia college. In that rather conservative milieu there were two faculty members who were ostracized by the rest of the faculty because one was an atheist and the other an agnostic. The Methodist chaplain told me he defended in public their right to be who they were, figuring that our Lord was one who would care for the outcast.

On one occasion, as he was walking off campus, the two ostracized faculty members were driving by, saw him, and stopped and picked him up. As he settled back in the car, the two faculty members began to kid about the irony of their defense by a clergyman. The atheist asked him, "You're rather strange. Just what are you?" Before the chaplain could reply, the agnostic spoke for him. "Don't you know? He is a living symbol!"

One could say that "by the mouth of babes and infants"—not to mention nonbelievers—"thou hast founded a bulwark . . . to still the enemy and the avenger" (Ps. 8:2). The priest is called to be a living symbol and not, as perhaps the agnostic implies, an empty symbol inducing us to participate in that which is not. There is a bridge—called the Sunshine Bridge—across the Mississippi River some miles south of Baton Rouge, Louisiana, built in the early 1960s as a political payoff. Its majestic four lanes come to an abrupt end in a cotton field—connecting a veritable "nothing" to the rest of the world. This is not the nature of the priest, for he is a living symbol joining the mystery of the abyss to the everyday world of people. The priest builds a bridge between two realities: humanity and the mystery from which God speaks.

In 1976, when a cross-section of parish search committees was asked what personal attributes and skills they wanted most in a priest, they replied a person of spiritual depth and, in the second instance, a capable preacher. Of course, these are vague categories: "spiritual depth" and a "capable preacher." But both are aspects of being a living symbol.

The connotation of depth is away from fads, superficial expectations, roles, and statuses, and in the direction of the primordial meaning of life, which extends beyond the immediate situation. The image of depth evokes the abyss. To preach well is to illumine the darkness of our personal depths from the depths of God's meaning. In all of this the priest is expected to be the hero, bearing the symbols of light and being the symbol himself. He preaches from the symbols.

This is a frightening demand laid upon the priest. Nobody enjoys being a living symbol for very long. I

was a member of the committee that prepared the
report for the 1976 General Convention. As our inter-
views of parish search committees progressed and a
trend developed, I related this to groups of priests with
whom I happened to be talking. A persistent resistance
to the findings was common. I told this to the chairman
of one parish search committee, who appeared to be a
quite gracious woman. Suddenly she bristled and said
very firmly, "You tell those bastards we mean it!"

People do indeed mean it, whether they are able to
express it or not. The priest is a messenger or, as the
original Greek put it, an angel. By what he says, by
what he does, and particularly by what he is, the priest
"catches" that awareness that lies amid and alongside
the mystery from which God speaks to humanity.
When the priest is effective he is this angel, this symbol enabling the coming-to-consciousness of God's vision for us all. His priesthood is the priesthood of
Christ, of whom it is said that "Christ shall give you
light" (Ephesians 5:14).

In recent years pastoral theologians have rightly observed that the root image of effective Christian ministry, including the priesthood, is service. But we must
be very careful not to reduce "service" to philan-
thropy or therapy. To be a living symbol is to serve
God's people at the heart of their need: to know God
as he knows them. This requires, however, that the
priest not shrink from the roots of his own power in the
receptive mode of the people's consciousness. To be
an effective priest is to serve in such a way that those
to whom we minister are made aware of the entire
breadth of their own meaningful world. In this alone is
freedom.

It is my intention to discuss the priest as angel or

symbol in five attributes of service. My approach here is more analytical than picturesque. In my book *Ministry and Imagination* the priest is described as mana-person, clown, wagon master, and storyteller, which was an effort to evoke images of the positive approach of the shamanistic roots of the priesthood. In an essay published in *To Be a Priest,* a collection edited by Robert Terwilliger and me, I spoke of the priest as the enchanter, which pointed to the need to recover the receptive mode of consciousness. In this present, more analytic approach, it is important to uncover the interaction between the priest and the community so that the community itself may know the presence of the living and active word among it, speaking from the fathomless ocean beyond our knowing.

For this purpose, keep in mind that the power of the priestly symbol lies in its ability to evoke a mythic and symbolic meaning latent within the members of the community who recognize this person as priest. This is projection, the process which is the first coming-into-consciousness of representations of experience which live very close to the person's own abyss. Such projections need to be handled with care so that they may point to the presence of God in the life of him who is doing the projecting, not just in the priest.

THE REALISTIC SERVANT

I could have called this "the humble servant," but we have a problem with the word "humble" in Christian and non-Christian circles alike. To be humble is to be realistic about ourselves, but humility carries with it no necessary judgment about the appropriate nature of that realism. A sentimental humility often affects stupidity, or incompetence, or ignorance, or ineptitude, or bad taste. This is not my meaning.

Humility has to do with knowing from whence we came and to what we shall return: the earth (*humus*). We are not like florists' flowers artificially forced to bloom without roots, which we know all too well are sham and soon to fade. True humility is a firm rootedness. As priests with our roots in the receptive mode, we can perceive ourselves as a valued symbol without having to prove ourselves by the standards of the action mode. We can share an intentionality with God for his purpose, in which we need be neither passive nor presumptive. Humility has to do with an awareness of both our sacramentality as priests and our active participation in the end which we serve for God.

I know a very fine priest who is a spiritual partner of mine. We talk with each other about our experience of God and our search for a more intimate knowledge of him. One day my friend said to me, quite ingenuously, "You know, I am puzzled. Things just seem to be happening in our parish. We dedicated a new church this month and it is all paid for. Our budget last year was $33,000, we hoped to increase it to $38,000, and we raised in pledges $42,000. We did all this without the usual campaign and with our largest donor leaving in a huff. Why do you think this has happened?"

The answer is because God wants this to happen, and also because the priest lets it happen. He does not let an egocentric style of priesthood get in the way. My friend is not unusually bright or prepossessing. As a preacher he is mediocre. But he is real. Authenticity shines through him unobscured, for he does not need to appear to be anything but himself, warts and all. Of course, there is more there than warts—there are

values. The ones he stands for are all too rare; he suffered for them in the world in which he was reared, a
world that values an extra dollar above all else.

In Greek mythology Chaos is the father of Gaea,
Mother Earth, and the grandfather of Zeus and Hades.
These two brothers, Zeus and Hades, are gods of the
action mode, and came into prominence as the evolution of human consciousness past to the action mode.
Zeus is the god of light, who represents the controlling
power, the hero who has slain Typhon, the youngest
child of Gaea. Hades is the god of darkness and the
dead, a place dreadful in its utter banality because it is
the dark side of the action mode. The priest, rooted in
the earth, speaks from the world of relationship to both
the light and darkness of the divided world of the action mode, Zeus and Hades. What the priest represents
in this sense is not explanation, but description; not
knowledge, but understanding. He offers those archetypical images that counterbalance the evolution of
human consciousness represented in Zeus and Hades.

To be humble, to be rooted in the earth, one has to
have self-esteem. There is nothing more ineffective
than a priest who needs constant reassurance. The
shaman had no assurance except the belief that the
spirits thought enough of him to speak through him.
There was no parish structure, no canon law, no pen-
sion fund, no status within the social system to tell him
that he was somebody. It was the spirits that told him
that and it was enough.

Self-esteem is different from egocentricity. An effective priest who is realistic about himself finds that
an overweening concern for his ego prevents that kind
of detachment which lets people see him as he is.
Egocentricity is very much of the action mode of

thought. It prevents that kind of vulnerability which enables people to see us without the feeling that somehow they are voyeurs. One of the finest compliments ever paid me was after a parish weekend I had led on sexuality, when a woman commented to me that I had talked and joked about sex without making them feel it was dirty. Perhaps this was because we figuratively "got naked together." It was like an experience I once had on a nude beach, where the sight of hundreds of naked bodies—some gorgeous, some ugly— was not so much titillating as strangely moving.

The realistic servant can risk the vulnerability that comes; he must "get naked" with those to whom he ministers. A priest, a friend, told me of a troubled young man who came to a discussion group the priest was leading. For more than an hour he thwarted through inappropriate remarks everything the priest tried to do. After the session the priest invited him into his office. His desk was customarily piled high with the accumulated untended business of running a parish. For a few moments they looked at each other across the desk, and then with one sweep of his arm the priest sent all the papers on the desk crashing to the floor. "Are you crazy?" asked the young man. "Not really," was the reply. "Then what do you want?" he asked again. "To talk honestly," the priest said; and talk they did about the depths of that primordial world which was struggling to be known in this young man's life.

The vulnerability of the realistic servant requires that we be comfortable with our own ignorance of God. We must push aside the facade of omnicompetence, the Zeus and Hades, and let ourselves embody the receptivity of Mother Earth. The professional model lays heavy emphasis upon knowledge and competence. While knowledge and competence are highly commendable in their place, the action mode, it is important that the priest lay equal emphasis upon understanding and sacramentality, characteristic of the receptive mode. The sacrament always points to that over which it has no control, but of which it is strangely expressive. This is different from the connotation of competence. The priest serves a mystery, in which he is rooted and which feeds his life of service, but which cannot be apprehended in its own terms.

THE SERVANT OF CHANGE

One expectation that some people have of the priest is that he has the power to change things. Iveson Noland, the Episcopal Bishop of Louisiana who died in a plane crash in 1975, loved to tell the story of when he was a chaplain on a troop ship in World War II. They were preparing for the invasion of one of the Pacific islands; it was very hot and dry, the troop ship was crowded, and the stench of unwashed, sweaty bodies packed together was unbearable. Some of the men who knew there was only one possibility for a bath came to him one Sunday and said, "Chaplain, would you pray for rain at the service today?" He did, and that night the damnedest typhoon hit that anyone could remember. The next morning he got a summons from the commanding officer. "Chaplain," he said, "no more messing with the weather!"

Our tendency is to see life as stable and to understand change as the exception. For premodern humanity the cycles of the seasons, the permanence of the social system, and its relationship to the land along the same relationship of its ancestors promoted a sense of permanence, although they may not have been quite as naive as we about this. Modern humanity with the notion of predictability, of which Newtonian physics is paradigmatic, has found the same expectation of permanence and predictability in the scientific world-view. It may be that quantum mechanics is making us more aware of the instability and unpredictability of the molecular structure of matter itself. Actually, the one thing of which we can be sure is that nothing is permanent. Change is the universal interpretation of experience which holds in all situations.

The issue is the relation of the priest to change. This is an important question, because the priest is often expected to be the stable center in the midst of a world of change, and yet he is somehow expected to be able to change things. Perhaps that apparent contradiction can be resolved if the priest is committed to *purposeful change*, to a teleological or eschatological or goal-oriented interpretation of the flux of life.

Remember that the shaman by his actions, words, and being lifts the consciousness of those whom he serves to a new level of awareness. He "blows their minds." In raising consciousness he changes their reality. He looks different. He does this because of his faith that in descending into the abyss, the "cloud of unknowing," he becomes infused with a vision that he must share.

Some worshipers at the shrine of ecclesiastical change see it only in terms of the action mode of knowing. I knew of a priest who was at the forefront of all the movements: ecology, women's liberation, gay activism, the peace movement, and so forth. He had a very deep ideological commitment, to the point that his conversation was so predictable that, save for the ensuing boredom, it was fun to "push his button" just to marvel at his consistency. What puzzled this priest was his complete inability to get the church excited about what he said. The clue to why he never could light a spark of enthusiasm for his causes in others lay in his fear of the erotic. Mention sex in an uncontrolled manner, as in an anecdote or an account of one's own experience, and he would insist that the subject be changed or he would leave. Women found him ideologically impeccable but unable to relate to their femininity. He was afraid to the verge of panic of the receptive mode, which was why all his pronouncements lacked excitement and vision.

The ability to effect change in a purposeful manner is related to our willingness to live in the receptive mode. It is helpful to reflect on the profundity of this profound point by exploring the "mystery of synthesis." C. G. Jung wrote about it in what he thought his crowning achievement: *Mysterium Coniunctionis: An Inquiry into the Separation and Synthesis of Psychic Opposites in Alchemy.* Some of his most ardent admirers find this work extremely puzzling, and his critics often use it to demonstrate his mental instability. To reduce a very complex history to a few sentences: for seventeen hundred years alchemy argued that life is a series of paradoxes or opposites. Whereas life sprang from primal matter or undifferentiated chaos of the abyss, it now exists both materially and spiritually in a series of debilitating unsynthesized opposites—e.g. masculine/feminine, reason/intuition, light/darkness, innovation/conservatism. Redemption is the synthesis of these opposites. Alchemy taught that

this redeeming synthesis could be achieved by finding
the "philosopher's stone," which is to be drawn from
undifferentiated chaos. The "stone" is sometimes a
liquid, sometimes a solid. Alchemy was concerned
with change, but a change into wholeness for humankind and the rest of creation. The key to change was the
stone.

Jung believed that alchemy was an expression of the
human collective unconscious. Alchemy's symbols,
which incidentally take shape in the zoomorphic form
common to the receptive mode, are archetypical images. The stone was identified with the Latin god
Mercury, who also gave his name to quicksilver, a very
ambiguous substance. He is related to the Greek god
Hermes, from whom we get the theological term her-
meneutics, meaning proclamation or interpretation.
Both Hermes and Mercury are gods of revelation.
What humankind seeks is illumination with its gift of
understanding; the stone symbolizes the means of that
illumination. Mercury is related to the mind and spirit,
and is identified with the Holy Spirit. It is this Spirit
which will teach us all things (John 14:26). Yet at the
same time there are strong parallels as well between
Christ and the stone (see especially 1 Peter 2:4–8). It is
the same Christ who also opens our understanding
(Luke 24:45).

The stone is the key to change. This notion of change
which effects synthesis, identified with a number of
archetypical images in the history of human consciousness culminating in the historical reality of Jesus of
Nazareth, is helpful as we explore the function of the
priest. Whether standing at the altar before the bread
and wine that become to us the body and blood of
Christ or sitting with a tortured soul that seeks light
amid darkness, the priest is expected to effect pur-

poseful change, rooted in the divine vision within the abyss itself. The priest then becomes identified with the historical images of humankind's receptive mode: Hermes, Mercury, the philosopher's stone, the Holy Spirit, and Christ himself.

It is worth noting in passing that while Mercury was considered androgynous—expressive of a synthesis of feminine and masculine symbols—Hermes was in Greek iconography identified by an erect phallus. Mercury represents the trickster, the bride, and is identified with the serpent. In other words, there is an erotic, androgynous ambiguity about the symbol—a union of eros and logos—which is worth the priest's reflection.

When the priest allows himself to be that symbol, he is a servant of change for the good. I well remember a graduating senior at Louisiana State University many years ago saying to me, "Thank you for all the changes you made in me!" This person came to LSU from a very small, backwater town. I had noticed he had changed for the better, but all I could say to him was, "What did I do?" His reply was, "It was not what you did, but that you were here." Somehow I was the philosopher's stone.

THE DISCERNING SERVANT

A third attribute of the effective priest who takes the receptive mode seriously is, ironically enough, a respect for reason and the trained intellect. In the third chapter it was pointed out that sensibility requires a disciplined mind as well as a willingness to enter the antistructure. The priest as hero ultimately leads us to rational consciousness.

Someone asked me not long ago if I did not agree

that the Cure d'Ars, whose name is St. Jean Baptiste
Vianney (1786–1859), was the model of the good
parish priest. This may strike the reader as a most re-
condite question, which perhaps testifies to the kind
of company I keep. As a matter of fact the Cure d'Ars is
the patron saint of parish priests, and so the question
had some basis in hagiology—although the inquirer
was in fact seeking to score a point against the value of
seminary education. As some will recall, the Cure
d'Ars flunked out of seminary, but according to his
biographer was ordained because he loved people and
had common sense.

I am sure that the Cure d'Ars was a very holy man
and I do not wish to bring judgment upon the deci-
sions of times other than my own in terms of contemporary values; but more harm has been done by ordaining persons who were dim-witted but "loved
people" than just about anything else, because
they lack the discipline that the discerning servant
must exert.

In the South what we call the "good ole boy" bears a
certain resemblance to the Cure d'Ars. He has a kind
of native cunning. I can think of more than one priest
who has been ordained with those who knew him best
justifying the ordination by saying that he was a "good
ole boy." Somehow such people make very poor
prophets and rather good anti-Christs. They are little
more than cultural flunkies. For example, where were
the "good ole boys" when Martin Luther King was
writing his famous letter from the Birmingham jail? I
suspect some of them were the addressees. How
many "good ole boys" are willing to challenge
the sentimentality of marriage and burial customs in
American culture? They are more likely to be making

peace, when there is no peace, with the "wedding consultants" and the Masons. What "good ole boy" has the wisdom, as well as the courage, to stand up in his pulpit and call in question the patently self-serving arguments of some in such areas as the Panama Canal treaty, the energy crisis, and the cost of medical care? The selves those arguments serve are more likely to be their drinking buddies.

I recall a number of years ago a person who was recommended to his bishop for ordination by a seminary with the comment that he was not very bright, but was a "good ole boy." I have not seen him in years, but rumor has come my way that this particular student was last seen spending considerable energy trying to distribute his sexual favors among members of his parish in such a way as not to create envy and disrupt his cure.

The effective priest is one who has acquired some distance from his feelings and can enable others to acquire the same distance from theirs. We are too ready to ridicule the desert Fathers who taught *apatheia*, meaning literally "un-passion." Maybe they have a wisdom to teach. The need to be needed, the compulsion to be right, the tingle of an infatuation, or acute discomfort in the face of change are examples of feelings that can victimize and destroy us. Sentimental irrationality, of which I wrote in the last chapter, cannot free us from such feelings.

The dangers are just as great with feelings of piety as they are with feelings of passion. It needs to be said once and for all to those who protest the speculations of the theologian, on the grounds that we should not complicate "the simple gospel of Jesus," that there is no such thing as the "simple gospel"! Such persons are pietists, victims of an endemic disease of the spirit which reaches epidemic proportions every so often. Pietism has never understood that what it takes for the "warm feeling of God's presence" can be a demonically seductive invitation to inhumanity. Such feelings can destroy us and, worse, they can destroy others. The pious feelings that emerge from any prayer group can be a smoke screen for the devil. We have to discern the spirits.

St. Paul wrote to the Corinthians, "The man who lives for his soul does not receive the things from the Spirit of God, for they are foolish to him, and he is not able to understand them, because he does not discern them in his spiritual self" (2:14, translation mine). The word "to discern" means to make a close, critical judgment. In the philosophy which prevailed at the time of St. Paul, humankind was thought to have three parts: body, soul, and spirit. The intellect was related to the spirit, whereas feeling was located in the soul. St. Paul says it takes the intellect to understand what is of God.

This is hard work. The biblical prototype of one that does this work is the Jewish wise man or sage. In the Book of Daniel, written in the second century B.C., the resurrection of the dead is being described. We are told that "those who are wise shall shine like the brightness of the firmament; and those who turn many to righteousness, like the stars for ever and ever" (12:3). The rhetoric is Jewish parallelism. The wise man is the one who turns people to righteousness. Daniel is described as a "professional wise man" in the court of King Nebuchadnezzar of Babylon. In fact, he underwent three years of special training (Daniel 1:15). Shades of seminary!

We are reminded of the three wise men or magi in Matthew's gospel (2:1). The evangelist probably had Persian astrologers in mind. Wise men include diviners, sorcerers, magicians, and interpreters of dreams as well as astrologers. Undoubtedly there was much abuse of the profession, but it would be a gross error to write all wise men off as charlatans. We probably have too narrow an understanding of what constitutes wisdom in this late twentieth century.

To return to Daniel, the author of this book shares with the author of IV Maccabees (one of the writings in the Pseudepigrapha dating from the time of Christ) the belief that the reason of the wise man overcomes passion. We need to remember this was the time in the history of human consciousness when the self was identified with the rational mind over against the feelings. For reason to overcome passion requires that the disciplined intellect, as already suggested for the discerning servant, save us from being victimized by our feelings. But wisdom for IV Maccabees is education in the Law, and this can appear to be a passionless escape into the action mode—although rationalism is a form of passion in itself. Perhaps it was the rigidity born of such an education that St. Paul, who was schooled in the same tradition, rails against when he ridicules the wisdom of the wise (1 Corinthians 1:18–25). The wise man can make an idol of his wisdom in order to have something behind which he can hide his passion. In the sixth chapter I shall point out that it is hidden passion that prevents eros, which is of the receptive mode, from leading us to God.

A solution to this danger of idolatry lies in being aware that wisdom in the Old Testament and Apocrypha is feminine. She has her roots in the receptive mode. She is more an oracle than a system—something like the Delphic oracle—which means that she can never be controlled. We can only participate in her and share in her enigmatic revelations. This is what is meant when it is said the priest is more than a man of knowledge, he is a man of understanding. Likewise, the act of spiritual discernment is more an intuition than a logical reduction, although we ought not to despise the latter as long as we do not claim too much for it. The wise man does not "tell" as much as he opens the mind to options and their consequences. To be wise in this sense requires the recovery of the receptive mode. It is to be the archetypical image of the wise old man, the mystagogue who brings both enlightenment and ecstasy.

How do I make contemporary the biblical reflection on the discerning servant? This conflated illustration helps. Some years ago several denominations developed a program of leadership training, using the insights of social psychology. These leadership training laboratories were sometimes managed by wise men and sometimes by fools. In the latter case people were hurt, not helped. Those hurt included the typical pastor, who came home convinced he no longer loved his wife and should marry one of the women with whom he shared this ten-day experience of antistructure. Foolish advice to that pastor would be to support his rash decision, and to speak of the new morality and the collapse of monogamy. It would be equally foolish to report him to his bishop, who would not understand what happened because bishops' jobs can isolate them from the antistructure. The wise man would send him back into the antistructure, but this time with a wise companion, to help him identify the symbols and diabols. In this way wisdom could be found and the hurt could be healed. Such a counselor would be an angel.

THE LIMINAL SERVANT

The word "liminal" comes from the Latin *limines,* meaning "threshold." The folklorist Arnold van Gennap used the word to describe rites of passage in which the participants stand poised between two roles in a society . The anthropologist Victor Turner went on to describe a state of being "betwixt and between," or living on the edge of the antistructure. The threshold of which I speak here is marked by the "great river" in my analogy in the first chapter. The effective priest lives on both sides of the river—he is consciously bimodal in thinking.

Earlier I spoke of the priest with his desk piled high. That recalls another priest of whom I knew. Some years ago we, the "young Turks" who worked in the same city, used to make great fun of him. Every morning he came into his office, looked at the mess on his desk, rotated it 45 degrees, and departed. He was totally disorganized, and his secretary was not much better. Yet he had the most amazing ministry, which almost made up for its total lack of intellectual discipline. It was not because of his preaching, liturgics, or teaching—all of which would lead a seminary faculty to despair. He bumbled, but he was loved. He made repeated mistakes, but they seemed to turn into success. He was opinionated, but without guile. He had a gift for success, even though he never tried for it. Forty years my senior, and I never could beat him at golf!

You wonder what makes such a priest effective? He

was a liminal person. It may seem strange to expand on what I mean with such a leap, but Plato makes the point that there are two principles which explain humanity and the world: reason and necessity. Reason, *nous* in Greek, is of the action mode. In the second chapter we spoke of the nootype, the shaping of humanity's understanding by the intellect. Necessity, *ananke*, is feminine in Greek, just like wisdom (*nous* is masculine). This suggests that necessity is in the receptive mode. But necessity is more than simple compulsion or fate. It is the force of nature, the orectic demands, playing upon humankind. The "orectic demands" are the bodily appetites or desires. Orectic symbols are those most basic and universal to humankind: birth and death, sexuality and eating.

Plato goes on to say that necessity is also the "errant cause" (*to tes planomenes actias*—the same phrase from which we get "planet," the "wandering star"). An "errant cause" is the opposite of a planned, rational cause. It would be the channel of a purpose that lies beyond—say in the mind of God.

We know errancy in terms of the proverbial "knight errant," who wanders aimlessly out on an adventure seeking to save the chance damsel in distress. The knight errant is perhaps best remembered in Miguel de Cervantes' character Don Quixote, who appears to be a bumbling fool, an anachronism living in the dim light of an age of chivalry long past. But somehow Don Quixote's mistakes turn out to be the occasions for new insights or great good. He dies Alonso Quijano the Good. It is not so much his competence, but his open—some might say "empty"—mind that is the ground of the knight errant's success. Most Americans know Don Quixote in the popular musical *The Man of*

La Mancha, and have some idea that the knight errant is one who "dreams the impossible dream."

The liminal religious practitioner is the priest errant as well as the professional of the action mode. One definition of errancy is to be outside the established paths, to be a bit of a rogue. In the terminology of analytical psychology, it is to let the shadow out to play. Earlier I mentioned the Greek god Hermes, who, like the Latin Mercury, is the herald and trickster. He is a shadow figure, a god errant, who cannot conform. Yet he is the means of revelation, the angel, what we call a mystagogue. The mystagogue is the one who conducts the soul to Heaven. Hermes' home, if he has a home, is with eros in the wilderness of the antistructure. He is an archetypical image for the liminal priest.

What does it mean to be a priest errant? Dennis Bennett, one of the first leaders of the neo-Pentecostal movement, once described for me the difference between himself before the "baptism of the Holy Spirit" and afterwards as the difference between forever taxiing down the runway and finally taking off. Flying is not a bad image for the priest errant. One of the problems with some neo-Pentecostals is that when they "get up" and experience a little of the errant in life, they get scared and drop an anchor to the ground—e.g., doctrinal or biblical fundamentalism. We have to be willing to glide with the wind, Hermes, the Holy Spirit; we need to experience nature, what Victor Turner has called the orectic symbols; and we ought to dream the impossible dream.

I stop and I think of the half-dozen or so priests errant I know and there is very little they have in common except that they are liminal. The priest I described earlier possessed a kind of domesticated liminality. He was more eccentric than half-crazy in the eyes of the world. Eccentricity will do for lack of anything else. It is less painful, I suspect, than a genuine creative weirdness. The Don Quixotes of this world are very vulnerable. They have a hard time finding that niche in which they can function. Consequently, while individuals may respond with gratitude to the liminal servant, society itself often does a poor job of permitting such servants to function in peace.

Part of the problem may lie in the fact that such a priest is androgynous. The liminal servant by the fact of his bimodal knowing brings together both the masculine and feminine consciousness into a synthesis. The awareness of androgyny—the feminine and masculine consciousness active in one person—is as old as human self-awareness. Plato speaks of the myth of androgyny in the same dialogue in which he describes reason and necessity. Contemporary humanity has inherited many centuries of Judeo-Christian polarization of the sexual symbols, however, and the feminine has been suppressed by the concept of an exclusively masculine God. This is so obvious it is hardly a debatable point. Yet we know that effective priesthood requires that awareness which we attribute to the feminine self—e.g., nurturing, active passivity, and community building. If we can be intentional about the liminal servant it may be possible to begin to overcome this debilitating polarization.

THE AUTHORITATIVE SERVANT

There are two kinds of authority, external and internal. External authority, which will be discussed in the next chapter, uses coercion, even if it is only the power of persuasion through logic. Internal authority, the fifth component of effective priesthood, possesses power by virtue of the inner conversation with the symbols and diabols, which lie at the heart of humanity's consciousness and motivation. Such authority is as the authority of Jesus, which Mark tells us was unlike the authority of the scribes. The evangelist demonstrates what he means by Jesus' conversation with an "unclean spirit" that Christ orders out of a person (Mark 1:22–27). It should be no surprise to the reader by now that external authority is of the action mode and internal authority is of the receptive.

The Venice statement of 1976 of the Anglican/Roman Catholic International Commission makes the point that Christian authority is the perception of the authoritative word of Christ in the actions and words of Christians. The word of God is, as St. John of the Cross said, the effect upon the soul. For a priest to possess authority, therefore, he must be vulnerable to others. He must show his soul. The tragic irony is that the perversion of authority, against which so many rebel, comes out of the need to do just the opposite: to hide behind status within the institution.

The reaction against the external authority of the church has often resulted in abrogating the entire notion of authority. A whole generation of priests has been reared to think that they are "enablers" or "brokers" with no authority. Some strange misconception of theories of management—or democracy—has led us to teach non-management in the name of a participatory democracy. I became the dean of a seminary at the end (thank God!) of this era and can testify that the effect was only to call authority by some other name, a hopeless circumlocution. (Ideology is so exhausting!)

In a conversation with James Forbes, the dean of the Union Seminary chapel in New York, I was struck by what he said about the authority of the priest. Forbes is a black Pentecostal pastor, the son of a Pentecostal bishop. In a very kindly manner he pointed out that the black pastor does not suffer all the pangs of guilt over authority that plague the white pastor. He went on to say that unless the priest claims his authority the community loses its sense of purpose and direction.

It is noteworthy that Peter Wagner of Fuller Seminary in Pasadena, a well-known evangelical institution, says the same thing. Church growth is impossible unless its pastors exercise their God-given authority.

This authority is, of course, bestowed by the community. It is the authority and the power of which the prayer of consecration of a priest in the Proposed Book of Common Prayer (pages 533, 534) of the Episcopal church speaks, given by the consent of the congregation. Without that authority the priest cannot serve the community; but it is grounded in his inner life and is founded on a moral, not a juridical base. It is related to the priest's willingness to embody the Christian myth.

Ideally, the authority of the priest possesses elements of both the receptive and action modes of knowing. Yet obedience is given naturally and spontaneously to the wise and good person who fulfills the expectation of the community for leadership. It is not his by "divine right," but is his authority as a result of his commitment, his sacrifice, and his service to the community. This means, to paraphrase the words of Richard Baxter's hymn, that the authority of the priest is rooted in the fact that he asks of us to enter no darker rooms than he has gone into before.

Authority is not something we acquire by title, but

by the community's acceptance of our priesthood. In
the Episcopal Church we call the priest in charge of
a self-supporting congregation the "rector," which
means "ruler." I recall an English priest who once
came to a parish in an American diocese in the deep
South and found that he was having very little success.
This was at least attributable in part to his obvious
dislike for bathing. His solution for his dilemma, rather
than the shower, was to ascend the pulpit one Sunday
and begin his sermon with the words, "I am the rector,
which word, as you in America probably do not know,
means 'ruler.' This means that I am to rule and you are
to be ruled." The poor man did not last very long after
that telling homily and soon returned to England.

The titles of the priest which most generally
connote authority are "Father," "Parson," and
"Preacher," depending upon your tradition. In my
own tradition two things are usually done with the
title "Father," both of which illustrate how we miss
the point of the priest's authority. In some quarters in
the Episcopal church priests not only introduce themselves as "Father so-and-so"—which tempts me to
comment on the quaint first name—but will address
one another that way throughout meetings and even
cocktail parties. In other quarters one can only be
called "Father" in the spirit of jest. For my part it
seems a most appropriate name for someone whom we
have found to possess an inner authority by the power
of his humility, discernment, flexibility, and liminality.

Eugene Kayden, the English translator of the poems
of Boris Pasternak, told me shortly before his death that
every priest should read over and over the account
of Father Zossima in Dostoevsky's *The Brothers*

Karamazov. Father Zossima was an elder or starets, a Russian Orthodox holy man, whose authority lay in the purity of his heart, his ability "to think one thing." Dostoevsky says of him "He sometimes astounded and almost alarmed his visitors by his knowledge of their secrets before they had spoken a word . . . . He was always almost gay. The monks used to say that he was more drawn to those who were more sinful." What Dostoevsky pictures for us is a priest with inner authority, one that we should gladly call "Father."

The power of illumination is related to the power to command the attention of those we serve. If the priest is, like Jesus, to turn the reality of people upside-down, he must teach as Jesus did, with authority. But it is authority that moves from the east to the west, from the receptive mode to the action mode, from inside out.

SUMMARY

Some years ago I was in New York at a friend's apartment, where a number of people of his acquaintance joined us for dinner. One of my fellow guests identified himself as a priest from a western diocese in search of a job. I asked what went wrong in his parish. His reply was, "Nothing went wrong. It was all very good. I just ran out of tricks."

Being an effective priest is not having a "bag of tricks." As a matter of fact, in a study done of parishes that have shown the most dramatic growth—100 per cent or more—over a stated period of time, it was found that the tenure of the priest in charge was more than twenty-four years! One runs out of tricks long before the end of twenty-four years. But such a priest does become well known. You cannot wear a mask for that long. Sooner or later the quality of your faith will show, and when it does it is that which makes for the effective angel or demon, as we shall see in the next chapter.

- FIVE -

The Priest as Demon

FEW people are neutral about the clergy. The present bishop of the Episcopal Diocese of Northwest Texas delights in telling the story of his experience of anticlericalism in New York City. He tells about the day he was walking along a street wearing his usual clericals. As he came to an intersection he had to wait for a green light. There was an open manhole close by where he was standing. He saw that someone wearing a hardhat was working in the manhole. Almost by chance their eyes met and the man in the hardhat spoke. "I can see," he said, "just by looking at you that you are a godless son of a bitch!"

There is something very refreshing about such an honest confrontation. So many people put on their "going-to-church" mask when they meet a priest and never share their honest feelings with him. In fact, I suspect they often do not have the courage to admit those feelings to themselves.

In the mid-1950s when I had just started as the Episcopal chaplain to Louisiana State University it was my habit to call on students in the dormitories. Someone had told me this was important to do, but it was not long before I discovered it only reinforced the destructive power of the priest in the minds of the students. I once called on a girl to appeal to her not to marry a man she had met ten days before. She told me I had no right to invite myself into her life. The long-standing effect of my call was to close off any possibility of ministry to her when she returned to LSU five years later, divorced and with two small children. She made that point to me very clearly. All my continued presence evoked was guilt.

Guilt is often the feeling which people project onto the priest. With guilt comes deep anger. The call to end all dormitory calling for me was one occasion when my knock was answered by a young man, clad only in his shorts, with a can of beer in his hand. He took one look, gasped "Oh my God," whirled around, and leapt out of the window. Fortunately, his room was on the ground floor. I often wondered how I would have explained what had happened if he had been on the fourth floor of that dormitory. It was not the loving God of Jesus Christ that was represented in that call that day, but the angry father of this young man's unresolved Oedipal conflict.

Aristotle said that the man who lives outside the city—the action mode, in our terms—must be either a beast or a god! This is what I am saying. The priest lives outside the city, in the receptive mode, and he has his choice: to be an angel—if you will, a god; or to be a demon—a beast. The second possibility is our present concern.

The effective exercise of the priestly ministry requires the priest to be aware of the shamanistic roots of the priesthood, for there lies his power to attract the projections of the deep symbolic reality of the people he serves. A projection, may I remind you, is the normal and often healthy first step we may take toward bringing meaning to our consciousness, up from the unconscious reality which lies within each of us. In doing so, we project, throw that meaning forward onto someone else. Such projection is symbolic. But it can be diabolic, if the priest fails to understand that the priestly image is rooted in the receptive mode of thinking, or if he is unwilling to accept the responsibility for its implications. In such cases the priest exerts demonic effect upon those who come in contact with him.

The priest evokes a power; he clothes an energy which lies within the unconsciousness of humanity and is ultimately a creature of God. The Greek word for this power is *daemon*. From a related word, *dunamis*, we get words such as "dynamite" or "dynamic." Our natural tendency is to personify the power—"thrones or dominions or principalities or authorities" (Colossians 1:16)—as happens in the person of the priest. One such personification we get from the very name of the power *daemon* is, of course, "demon." Demons are the powers of darkness, the destructive clothing of this power.

What follows is an analysis of the demonic effect the priest may exert, based upon his shamanistic roots. I shall suggest four contexts in which a diabolic effect may take place, and illustrate them from my own experience. If in doing so I appear to call into question the sincerity or authenticity of the vocation of a number of clergy, it is not my intention. The problems are common to us all. They ought to be identified, but it would be gratuitous to pass judgment upon the vocation of anyone on the basis of anecdotal information.

The possibilities for the demonic effect in our priesthood must be carefully separated from the possibilities for failure. A Christian priest should expect failure so that it may not destroy his hope in the gospel. Failure is a result of the brokenness of this world and is the inevitable product of risk. The priest who never fails is the priest who never allows God to create a new wholeness through him. Whereas I would not go so far as to seek failure and despise success, it is true to say that the priest is called to be faithful, not successful.

The power of the priest belongs to him not because of external authority, as in professional accreditation, but because the priestly image is rooted in the consciousness of the receptive mode of knowing. Power in itself is neither good nor bad, but it can either destroy or create depending on what the person who has the power lets it do to him. It is very easy for the power to turn on us and catch us in the lust for power for its own sake. Power then becomes a goal rather than a means.

The turning in on ourselves of the priestly power can be a very deceptive process. The most blatant example which comes to my mind is the Inquisition of the late Middle Ages and early modern period. But such a "holier-than-thou" attitude can be far more subtle. A contemporary example of an equally dark expression of power in the name of Jesus is this. Shortly before Christmas in 1977 a plane crashed, carrying the whole basketball team of the University of Evansville in Indiana to their deaths. Shortly afterwards a friend of mine found himself sitting at dinner next to someone from Evansville, and my friend made a comment intended to share some sadness over the recent tragedy. "Oh no!" his dinner companion retorted. "That coach came from Oral Roberts University and those boys are singing sweet music with Jesus." To this demonic, cruel comment—the obvious implication being that if the coach came from some secular or, perhaps, Roman Catholic institution, there would be no "sweet music with Jesus"—my friend could only say, "I doubt that their parents feel that way."

The dark side of power seizes us whenever we hide from the full implications of the receptive locus of the priestly image. Self-surrender and ambiguity characterize the antistructure and they are to be treasured for the way in which they protect us from the misuse of power. When they are not present we fall into a reduction, of which I identify four categories. By "reduction" I mean the way the understanding of priesthood may be limited, constricted, or even distorted; I mean the way it may be "reduced" in effectiveness.

We need to be clear about how these four reductions relate to one another. The *functional reduction* is a denial of the receptive mode of consciousness in Christian living. It is ideological or rational in its approach and, when it degenerates, produces either sentimentality or cynicism. We are left exposed and undefended from the power of the antistructure. *Role reduction* is society's defense against the threatening power of the priest, effected by bestowing a reduced role upon the priest. It considers him silly, or even perverted. A degenerated functional reduction can cooperate with a role reduction. The *behavioral reduction* resists functional and role reduction, but cannot perceive the phenomena of the receptive mode in anything but action mode categories. This produces an oppressive caricature of the mystery of the priest. The *personal reduction* is more perceptive than the other three, but willingly uses the power of the receptive mode for its own demonic ends.

FUNCTIONAL REDUCTION

The first category of the demonic element in priesthood is a sociological reduction. It denies the symbolic role of the priest and finds its rationale in ideological commitment. It identifies the priest with what he does and limits his doing. He is divorced from the mystery of his own being. The priest refuses to be a sacrament of sensibility to the community and consequently the priest in the receptive mode functions with only an intentional relationship to the action mode. The effect is what I describe as functional reduction.

In June, 1977, in the professional supplement to the journal of the United Church of Canada entitled *Perspective*, Vernon Wishart attempted to explain the difference between the Catholic and the Protestant views of ministry. What he came up with was well thought out, but it was an example of functional reduction. He says that in Protestantism the minister is the servant of the Word, and his effectiveness has nothing to do with his person or being. It depends, rather, on whether or not "the gospel is proclaimed, heard, and acted upon" in what he does. This was Calvin's doctrine of ministry. Word is here totally of the action mode. Wishart's understanding of the Roman Catholic priesthood is that "the priest is the Word." It is he himself who bears salvation.

Wishart in this article is trying to explain why

Roman Catholics object to the ordination of women and Protestants do not object. It is intended as an irenic statement. The problem is that his distinction between Roman Catholicism and Protestantism does not hold, and where we attempt to live as if it does we are in trouble. What Wishart says about the Protestant understanding of ministry is equally true of the best Roman Catholic understanding, and what he says of the Roman Catholic doctrine of the priesthood is also true of the way the Protestant ministry functions. This latter truth has been made most vivid for me in conversations with Southern Baptist clergy, who have at least an intuitive grasp of bimodal consciousness.

One cannot divorce the Word a person serves from the person himself, with all that means for the receptive mode. The priest embodies the Word, including the inner Word we project onto him. What else does Phillips Brooks' famous definition of preaching as "truth mediated through personality" mean? Why else would those who think God is a cosmic prude expect their clergy to be equally prudish? I am sure that the people of Garneau United Church in Edmonton, where Wishart is pastor, are not indifferent to him as a person, bringing to them the promise of salvation. The issue of the ordination of women to the priesthood is not nearly as simple as Wishart implies.

One of the problems is that many people think it is. Herein lies an illustration of the demonic dimensions of functional reduction, in that it leaves us exposed to the power of the receptive mode. It is like taking LSD without knowing it.

There are those who have interpreted the debate over the ordination of women in the Episcopal church as solely an issue of women's rights, a question of justice within institutions. This is not only naive, it has frightening implications, because it blocks any awareness of the antistructural implications of women as priests. The presence of women priests will awaken the powerful image of the feminine, the Great Mother, in every person's mind.

The Great Mother, nourishing and devouring, has lain suppressed in the western unconscious as we saw in the second chapter. It would seem that ever since St. Paul preached against the silversmiths of Ephesus and their busy trade in the shrines of Artemis (Acts 19:23–41), Christianity has carefully suppressed the feminine symbol. I am not at all sure that the repression of the nature religions in the Old Testament, of which St. Paul's actions were a culmination, is an unqualified blessing. It seems clear from the irrational behavior of some opponents of women's ordination, as well as some protagonists, that unless we are aware of the implications of the archetypical image of the Great Mother within each one of us we run the risk of being "devoured" by her when she confronts us unaware.

I have been told of an occasion at a clergy conference in the Episcopal church when a woman was administering the chalice. She came to a priest, who grasped both the chalice and her hand, dug his fingernails into her flesh and muttered, "I hate you, you witch!" For whom in the presence of the precious blood does this man declare his hate? I suggest that it is not the woman administering the chalice but the unrecognized, unadapted Great Mother within him that is the witch, and he is devoured by that hate.

The same unadapted emergence of the Great Mother is evident in a priest who was quoted in the local newspaper as saying that all women priests are either lesbians or prostitutes. This is hardly a rational statement, but reveals the terror of the feminine symbol and of the receptive mode.

The professional model of ministry has at its worst moments supported the naiveté of functional reduction. It has implied that the priest is one who possesses certain skills—no more, no less—which he needs to exercise. Such a priest, if one takes this model literally, is left unprepared to meet the real expectations of those he is called to serve. Then disappointment would be the mildest reaction we might reasonably expect. It is like the occasional priest who refuses to hear someone's confession on the grounds of some ideological bias, without being aware that this person wants to talk to God through him.

A friend of mine, a Canadian naval chaplain, once told me about a particularly critical event in his ministry. He was serving on an aircraft carrier in the Caribbean. A friend of his, a pilot, was involved in a freak accident when the planes were being launched and before he could be fished from the sea the ship's propellers had severed a leg. The chaplain encountered his friend in the sickbay, still conscious, in terrible pain. His only words were, "Bill, make it stop hurting."

They are like the words a child would address to a mother, but they are the words to a priest. The priest is not seen as a technician. He is not a doctor with a syringe of pain-killing morphine. It would have been utterly inappropriate for the priest to reply as a professional. At that moment my friend became vividly aware of his function. Far better that he speaks as mystagogue, one who leads us into mystery. The priest is expected to be familiar with the mystery of pain, even more than a mother. He is the shaman who has fasted, who can walk through fire and lie submerged in ice-cold water. He is the one who has laughed in the face of death. It is to such a person that the wounded pilot cries out, "Bill, make it stop hurting."

Many people know the story of Carlos Castaneda's seduction from being a typical graduate student in anthropology to becoming an apprentice shaman. It is the account of the undoing of a functional reduction. Not nearly so many of us know Maya Deren's description of her possession by a Voodoo spirit, Ghede. In 1947 she went to study Voodoo religion in Haiti as the typical rationalist cynical social scientist. As she puts it, she discovered how vulnerable she was. It was not a matter of accepting a Voodoo metaphysics. What she experienced was a fact: she was possessed by a power clothed in a symbol or diabol. What Ghede did to her for good or evil depended upon whether she insisted or not upon a functional reduction of the meaning of her presence at that Voodoo ritual.

The priest is an instrument of possession, for good or bad, because he is both a subject of and an object for projection. Nothing can be more dangerous than to pretend otherwise. Like a policewoman posing as a prostitute, leading on her "John" until he tries to make a buy and then slapping on the cuffs, the priest who insists on acting only in an institutional role betrays people in their vulnerability. It is no wonder that they can become very angry at us.

ROLE REDUCTION

Functional reduction is how the priest understands what he does. It is to be an ideologue when people want a living symbol. Role reduction is how society sees what he does. This is to accept the illusion of secularism—to hold that all meaning is rational. It is often the way society deals with the threatening nature of the receptive mode.

In such a view the priest is the subject of many a caricature. Anthony Trollope writes in *Barchester Towers:*

> There is, perhaps no greater hardship at present inflicted on mankind in civilised and free countries, than the necessity of listening to sermons. No one but a preaching clergyman has, in these realms, the power of compelling an audience to sit silent, and be tormented. No one but a preaching clergyman can revel in platitudes, truisms, and untruisms, and yet.receive as his undisputed privilege, the same respectful demeanour as though words of impassioned eloquence, or persuasive logic, fell from his lips . . .
>
> With what complacency will a young parson deduce false conclusions from misunderstood texts, and then threaten us with all the penalties of Hades if we neglect to comply with the injunctions he has given us!

Trollope's priest stands in a time-honored tradition that stretches across the literary history of Christendom. There is an old French story "The Priest's Breeches," for example, which I know in its fourteenth-century form, that has roots as far back as the second century. It tells about a priest who, with his bishop's consent after the fact, cuckolds the local butcher. The priest is shown as crafty, with unmitigated gall, and devoid of the concern for the sacrality of the erotic.

Tennessee Williams, who once described his grandfather, an Episcopal priest, as the kindest man he ever

knew, has created in *Summer and Smoke* the Reverend
Mr. Winemiller, who destroys people with his kind-
ness. He contrasts him with Dr. Buchanan, who embodies a physical, primordial energy beloved by
Williams. The priest devoted himself to "worn-out
magic" and being his neurotic wife's keeper. His
weakness is malignant, as exemplified in its effect upon
his daughter.

The old French story, Trollope, and Williams are
examples of a continued portrayal of the priest as
weak, silly, and ineffective. Current television rarely
gets beyond this image. The typical cleric is middle-
aged, bald, soft, and easily shocked. He talks in a
stained-glass voice, sips tea, and is afraid of his
shadow (Jung might say "his Shadow"). He is a kind of
joke, a momentary giggle like the inappropriate, nervous laugh that runs through a theater during a profoundly moving scene. If we can get some distance on
that giggle we see how pitiful it is, how it glosses over
what threatens us. It is like a holy card someone once
gave me. It read, "All for Jesus, through Mary, with a
smile." The holy card sounds like a football cheer at
Calvary.

While this treatment of the priest may illustrate one
way in which society protects itself from a consciousness of the terror that a priest rightly symbolizes, many
clergy seem to derive some secondary gain from role
reduction. Their sentimentality, if not their cynicism,
derived from the functional reduction, hooks into society's reduction of the priestly role. Two examples
come to my mind.

In some seminaries it seems they must have a course
entitled "Hearty Masculinity 101." I am referring to a
whole repertoire of phony boyish camaraderie, joined

to a kind of faded Irish charm. It is something like a high-school football team getting itself worked up to run out onto the field. You may recall the pulled punches, the arms around the shoulders, the slaps on the buttocks, and the nervous exhortations to "hang tough."

This illustration should not suggest more than I want to say. Masculinity is a desirable quality within the priest, whether he be male or female. That logos or cosmic reason which is associated with masculinity is an important element in the life of the priest. But a deep and authentic masculinity requires as an inner counterpart an equally deep and authentic femininity. *Together* they awaken a profound, sensible consciousness. Androgyny requires and encompasses both.

The other illustration of intentional role reduction has to do with what my father called the "missionary grin." He had a particular dislike for revivalists—his grandfather was one—and he questioned their sincerity. The missionary grin is usually associated with a handshake that leaves you a candidate for the orthopedic surgeon. If you are confused about my referent, a quick glance at the Saturday afternoon paper, with its two-column advertisements on the religion page, will illustrate the point. One wonders before all those smiling faces what has happened to the ideal priest, who reveals in his demeanor sorrow for the sufferings of Christ.

What I am ridiculing is the easy substitution of sentimentality for sensibility. No one is going to crucify the local Irish curate because he roots for Notre Dame, or the visiting revivalist because he is against adultery, gambling, and drugs. The problem is that such priests leave us very little room for wrestling with our visions and our corruption. Like Alma, the daughter of Reverend Winemiller in *Summer and Smoke,* the only choice it leaves us is to cling to some stone angel or take up with the traveling man passing through.

There is no risk in such a priest. He plays up to our fear and our desire for assurance. What he offers is like "junk cereal." It tastes sweet, it gives us something to crunch on, and our appetite is appeased for the moment, while all the time we are dying from religious malnutrition. This lack of priestly nerve, cloaked behind a sugar coating, is demonic. It destroys people because it does not help them face the dark corners of their lives.

Again we recall the Pietists' and the so-called "simple gospel of Jesus Christ." So often, what is meant by the "simple gospel" is the "junk cereal." It does not touch the receptive mode of humanity's reality, much less the abyss within. It is sentimental and cannot effectively challenge the cynicism of our age.

What has happened to the priest who understood the salvific effect of tears? There is a long history in Christian spirituality of the necessity of appearing sad and in pain. Somehow such sorrow is more authentic. Sentimentality never loses control. Sensibility demands a surrender of self to the mystery of life's events. A priest who must control cannot bear the angelic message.

A friend of mine tells how he discovered this fact. He was the curate in a parish. On one hot summer afternoon, when he was the only priest on duty, word came that the only child of a couple he knew as close friends in the parish had been killed. They had longed to have children for years before the birth of this son.

Now in his own front yard the child was dead under the wheels of his father's car. The young priest drove to that house, fervently praying that God would make him equal to this task. He entered the house, walked to the parents' bedroom, and went in to find them sitting on the edge of the bed, clinging to each other. The blood of his son was still on the father's trousers. Before the priest could speak he broke into sobs—long, uncontrollable weeping. He could only gasp for breath. This went on for a long time before he was able to utter a single coherent sentence. I know of no pastoral counseling manual that says: "First weep uncontrollably." Some would say that my friend had "blown it." I would agree with the couple, however, who told this priest some weeks later that there could be no more effective ministry than what he had done. He had entered with them into the mystery of death, fought the demons and found the angels.

BEHAVIORAL REDUCTION

In my travels about the country I met an assistant priest in a parish I was visiting who asked me what seemed to be a curious question. "Is the priest," he inquired, "a 'professional Christian'?" I had to confess I had never heard the term. He went on to explain that the pastor of the parish, who is an extremely talented man, had questioned his conduct on one occasion because, as his superior had explained, it is the task of the priest to be the "professional Christian."

Other than to suggest that this term should be offensive to every baptized person, I could only ask the young priest to explain what he thought it might mean. It turns out that to be a "professional Christian" is to be predictably "straight," conservatively dressed in neat, good-quality black suits, to comb your hair and polish your shoes, never to take more than two drinks at a party, and to speak with authority in all matters of religion. In other words, it is to fulfill an image guaranteed to please a calling committee made up of the most unimaginative people in the parish, whose highest priority is never to be embarrassed or surprised.

Behavioral reduction reduces the shamanistic roots of the priesthood to the univocal behavior of the action mode. It suppresses the feminine spontaneity that should pervade the priesthood, burns all the bridges and sinks all the boats that could carry us back across the great river within our consciousness toward the east and the fathomless ocean. The "professional Christian" is the banal, safe, predictable priest, the opposite of the liminal servant. In behavioral reduction the internal authority of the receptive mode is reduced to the external authority of the action mode.

This notion of the "professional Christian" is very different from functional and role reduction. The behavioral reduction of the priesthood acknowledges that symbol and myth are central in religion, but defines religion conceptually and systematically so that it becomes controllable. It has a compulsive need to keep everything "clean." It is particularly common among the more Catholic-minded Christians who are very quick to despise Protestantism. It presents us with a fondness for church, priesthood, and sacraments, but strangely encased in a univocal straitjacket. Behavioral reduction claims the mystery for itself, but its understanding of mystery is to religion what Sir Walter Scott's novels were to the Middle Ages. Without all the ambiguity, all the tension between cruelty and devotion, all the risk, all the genuine humanity, only a caricature remains.

Behavioral reduction is concerned with the externals of the church's teaching. Hermes and Mercury are strangers to its world. Orthodoxy is readily measurable, and anyone who does not fit into its procrustean bed is tolerated if considered uninformed, or vilified if believed educated. I speak from much experience. There are the entering seminarians who come having memorized their pastor's catechism by which they judge the faith of their faculty. Much worse, there are the clergy who test the recent graduates of our seminaries by asking questions for which there is the only one possible correct answer: the one within their private catechism. The result in many Episcopal seminaries is a non-credit *ad hoc* course on using the right words with the priests back home.

In one instance a priest who held a powerful post within a diocesan system prevented the ordination of a seminary graduate on the grounds that he lacked a spiritual life. The irony of that was that the graduate had come to seminary out of the charismatic movement, never missed daily service, made his communion several times a week, and led a prayer group. If anything, he was excessively pious. The problem was that his daily devotional schedule was not the same as the priest's and consequently not that which the priest believed absolutely necessary for an authentic prayer life. The seminary graduate did not do the right things at the right time.

Obviously we do not judge the effectiveness of our belief or our actions by some one prescribed, single system. The ground of the Christian life is the mystery of God's self-disclosure to the world, which is most intimately and powerfully known in symbol and myth. These can and inevitably do beget many systems of belief and practice. My own Anglican tradition assiduously avoids committing itself to any one way. In fact, the presuppositions of behavioral reduction are no less naive as regards theological methodology than the presuppositions of those who are convinced the stork brings babies. It fails to understand the whole process of theological "gestation."

I am convinced that we can account for the demonic nature of behavioral reduction only by concluding that it meets a psychological need to protect our outer appearance from the dark, subterranean self. My experience has led me to be leery of a rigid, righteous proclamation of moral standards, because so often the very people who make them follow a style of life which is in direct contradiction to what they profess. Some would call this hypocrisy. I would be more inclined to think that it is related to a need to keep the purity of their souls unsullied by the lust of their bodies. Their doctrine of man is Cartesian, if not docetic. The rationalization of their own conduct is in some ways quite unconscious.

For example, I grew up in a rather average Episcopal parish. My rector, who baptized me, suffered from Parkinson's disease. The last time he was present in the sanctuary of my home parish was to present me for ordination to the diaconate. He was a rather quiet man, whom I never knew very well. His patient endurance of his suffering and delightful subtle sense of humor were perhaps his most distinguishing features to me.

I was rather surprised to discover, therefore, that

this humble, quiet man gave as ordination gifts an em-
bossed certificate which might seem like the most ar-
rogant statement you could imagine. Written by the
nineteenth-century French Dominican Lacondaire, it
reads in part:

> To live in the midst of the world without wishing its
> pleasures;
> To be a member of each family, yet belonging to none;
> To share all sufferings;
> To penetrate all secrets;
> To heal all wounds;
> To go from men to God and offer Him their prayers;
> To return from God to men to bring pardon and hope;
> To have a heart of fire for charity and a heart of bronze
> for chastity;
> To teach and to pardon, console and bless always
> My God, what a life!
> And it is yours, O priest of Jesus Christ!

Viewed from the action mode, this statement is absurd. Margaret Bowers, a psychiatrist who has done
much study of the clergy, said about a statement very
much like this one that any priest who believed this
had to be psychotic. I assume she meant "psychotic"
in the destructive sense, since what I advocate could
be called a "creative psychosis." But I wonder if to
believe Lacondaire is to be destructively psychotic.
A seminarian gave me a copy of this quotation recently
and his explanation of why he liked it was not particularly articulate, but it was not psychotic. Furthermore,
I am confident my rector was anything but destructively psychotic.

The point is that if one takes this proclamation literally as a systematic analysis of the priest, it is an exam-

ple of behavioral reductionism at its worst and, as I have suggested, may be symptomatic of psychopathology. If one sees it, however, as a Gallic groping for the role of the priest in the receptive mode, you can understand why people like my gentle rector admired it. It is clearly excessive in any man's language and it is not to my taste. But the difference between arrogance and a certain creative weirdness lies in what you make of that excessiveness.

PERSONAL REDUCTION

We are all familiar with the person of Simon in the Acts of the Apostles, who asked if he might purchase the gift of the Holy Spirit that he might share in the power of Peter and John. Despite the fact that he gave his name to "simony," the selling of ecclesiastical offices, the story has a happy ending. Simon repented in the face of Peter's invective (Acts 8:9–13, 18–24).

The recognition of the power of the priestly image and its use to further our own ends did not end with Simon, nor is it simply a matter of paying for ordination. I think we know this and we do not have to belabor this category very long. The significant issue for this study is that it means we must recognize for our own health the symbolic power of the priest and his ability to evoke the strong feelings of others; otherwise we distort or reduce the personal, hence commit personal reduction. Personal reduction is a self-centered, malevolent misuse of the receptive mode.

The most obvious form of personal reduction or conscious diabolism is sexual. I have alluded to John Updike's novel *A Month of Sundays*. This novel is only

one, the only *good* one, among a number I could name
that celebrate the extramarital exploits of the clergy.

But there is a side to conscious diabolism which is
less titillating than amorous adventurism and a great
deal more subtle. It is the appropriation of the positive
projections for ourselves, the delight in our own importance. It is not hard to do.

For example, I do more than my share of parish
weekends, diocesan conferences, and special provin-
cial programs. People come to those occasions expectant,
eager, and hopeful. They are generally very vulnerable. It is like the nineteenth-century camp meeting.
With a little skill in storytelling, a dozen good records
and a hi-fi, and a sense of timing, it is possible to evoke
a response in which *you* are the end not the means.
What scares me is that I can guarantee a standing ova-
tion at the close. God gets lost very early in all of this. I
have a certain sympathy for those who wear hair-
shirts to overcome their pride.

How does someone who is in the public eye and
suddenly recognizes his power within the community
maintain his balance and know without a doubt that
the power is not his, but belongs to the people and to
God? I hope we are all embarrassed when deference is
paid to us, never thinking it is our due. My first experience with those who did not was witnessing a priest
who was a student at my seminary arguing with a
Jewish pharmacist at the corner drugstore who failed
to give him a ten per cent discount on a tube of tooth-
paste. I shall never forget my embarrassment.

I will spare you my feelings about clerical discounts
and those who solicit them, and even more the salaries
that make us into beggars if not pickpockets; but I
think they too contribute to personal reductionism. It

is important that a priest never turn down a gift, no matter how poor the giver. It is equally important that he never expect a gift and never manipulate the situation to bring it about.

A very subtle form of personal reduction is a self-righteousness that edges over into personal messianism. We can never avoid completely the cult of the personality in the church. In fact, it is not desirable that we do. But it has to be joined to a humility which prevents us from advertising the local preacher instead of God. Conservative Protestants are particularly guilty of the exaltation of Dr. So-and-so to the Godhead. The silk suits, the well-polished television presence, and the identification of the congregation by the pastor's name all help with this confusion of the priest and the deity.

There is something almost psychopathic in the personal reduction. Its practitioners are the demonic con men. I was talking recently with a friend, whose upbringing had been as a Baptist in a small southern town. We were discussing a well-known itinerant priest-evangelist, who has a considerable reputation for doubling the size of congregations almost overnight. But to what end? My friend had recently seen him perform, and commented on the slickness of what he saw, as the evangelist moved from the Bible to the piano and back again. There was nothing here in the action mode. There was no scholarship and little theology. It was all in the receptive mode; but my friend could only report a feeling of growing revulsion. He had seen it countless times before as a child, perhaps not as polished. People were being seduced—not into holiness, but into statistics, each just one more head to be counted.

Sometimes it is society itself that traps us in such a diabolism, however. I recall once, when I was Episcopal chaplain at LSU, standing in line in a ticket office to get two tickets for the Sugar Bowl. There were at least three hundred people ahead of me. The assistant ticket manager, who was a friend of mine, looked from his window and saw me—I am hard to miss in a black suit at 6′6″—and called, "Father, don't stand back there. These people won't mind if we serve you first!" They "minded" a lot! I remember the looks, and I wonder how many souls I lost for Christ that day.

SUMMARY

Primitive humankind through its shaman possessed an immediate sense of the spirits' presence. It recognized readily that the shaman was a channel of power. It knew that what he said came to primitive humankind out of the mystery of life itself. Whether for good or bad, it was dependent upon the shaman's power. We are inclined now to consider how sad was humankind's lot, for it had no other source of ultimate meaning in life than the manipulations of the shaman. Probably its plight was not as poor as we imagine, and in some ways they may have been better off than we are.

We have lost our innocence, however. It was not too long ago that a mother drew me aside after preaching in her parish and said, "Please talk to my son. He wants to be a priest. I know it is all right for some people [she could have added, "like you"], but not Jim. He has too much promise to waste his talents." Have we in our secular, disenchanted minds, come to think of what the priest does, as a waste of time? The four reductionisms we have described may lead us to say yes, but they arise out of a secularized, disenchanted world.

If only we could see that in fact these reductions of the priest point to more than a waste of time. Granted, what a priest does is often destructive—but if so, it is because there is a power in what the priest is within a community. It is power not his own, a power which he must not claim as his own. When seen for what it is, this power can be amazingly creative rather than destructive. It is the power of God.

- SIX -

A Theology of Priesthood

THEOLOGY is the answer to the question of the experience of God: What does it mean? It is a conceptual and systematic response, a function of the action mode of thinking. Prior to such thinking meaning there is felt meaning, which constitutes the necessary transition between experience and a conceptual response. Theology seeks to clarify the meaning of the experience so that we may share the experience with our contemporaries and those who have gone before. The purpose of this chapter is to clarify and share the meaning of the experience of the priest with the Christian theological community of the present and the past.

The religious community makes a statement about the meaning of its ministry. A vivid illustration of this occurred to me in the United Air Lines lobby at JFK airport in New York. I was waiting there when a troop of young men appeared in the lobby. There was something about them that looked strange. Their ears protruded. After a few seconds I realized that it was because of their haircuts. Their coiffure was about twenty years out of date, only their hairstyle was all the more obvious because of the patch of white skin that abutted their hairlines and called attention to the longer, more fashionable hair that had been there until a day or so before.

Who were these people? At first I thought they were Marine recruits, particularly when someone began barking out the roll. They had that air of new enlistees. They looked both frightened and excited. But their hair was really not short enough for that, and I noticed their attire. Each young man was dressed in a conservative, blue suit, with a tie of the same color, and a white shirt. For a moment, since I was standing in an international airport, I thought maybe they were a group of English choirboys; but I dismissed that on realizing that they were too old and that there was a girl or two among them. Dying of curiosity, I found an excuse to come closer, and then I saw they wore identifying labels. They read: "L.D.S." Latter-Day Saints! These were Mormons, beginning their two-year required service as missionaries.

Their appearance is a theological statement of the Mormon understanding of ministry. As someone else once described Mormon missionaries, they were devout and defensive. Nothing could look more "square," more devoid of risk than these young people. They represent a society committed to the nineteenth-century puritan ethic: no gambling, no drinking, and no sex outside a marriage which is carefully planned shortly after their return from the missionary tour. This prescribed appearance should not surprise us, when we recall that the most complete genealogical records in the world are stored in caves carved in the mountains above Salt Lake City. It bespeaks a people whose whole intention is to have the past, present, and future under control.

Of course, there is good precedent for theological statements about the priesthood in the attire of the church's representatives. Roman Catholics, Eastern Orthodox, Episcopalians, some Lutherans, and occasional other Protestants wear special clothing. The irony is that in the late twentieth century we have come to miss the point, which is itself indicative of the confusion over the priesthood. A different *style* of dress—namely, the clerical collar as opposed to a shirt and tie—is relatively new in the Christian tradition. It is more of a uniform—i.e., a statement that "this is a priest"—than what has more precedence in history, a different *mood* of dress. The priest has for centuries worn the same style as some non-priests, but with more somber tones. Clerical attire was not so much a uniform as a theological statement about the priesthood. Johnny Cash in describing why he wears black tells us what that statement is.

Well, you wonder why I always dress in black.
Why you never see bright colors on my back.
And why does my appearance seem to have a somber
    tone?
Well, there's a reason for the things that I have on.
I wear the black for the poor and the beaten down
living in the hopeless, hungry side of town.
I wear it for the prisoner, who has long paid for his
    crime
but is there because he's a victim of the time.
I wear the black for those who've never read
or listened to the words that Jesus said
about the road to happiness through love and charity.

Why do you think he's talking straight to you and me?
Well, we're doin' mighty fine, I do suppose,
in our streak-o-lightning cars and fancy clothes.
But just so we're reminded of the ones who are held
    back
up front there oughta be a man in black.
I wear it for the sick and lonely old,
for the reckless ones whose bad trip left them cold.
I wear the black in mourning for the lives that could
    have been.
Each week we lose a hundred fine young men.
And I wear it for the thousands who have died,
believing that the Lord was on their side.
I wear it for another hundred thousand who have died,
believing that we all were on their side.
Well, there's things that never will be right I know,
and things need changing everywhere you go.
But 'til we start to make a move to make a few things
    right,
you'll never see me wear a suit of white.
Aw, I'd love to wear a rainbow every day,
and tell the world that everything's OK;
But I'll try to carry off a little darkness on my back.
'Till things are brighter
I'm the man in black."

Give me the Mormon missionaries and Johnny Cash
over the brightly colored clerical shirts some priests
wear these days. The latter are an anomaly, setting the
priest apart and yet contributing nothing to the power
of the gospel message. Better a symbol or nothing at all
rather than an empty sign. But whether or not we wear
our theology "on our sleeve," we need to be clear at a
conceptual level as to what the priesthood means. It is
to this conceptual tradition that we need to look, in the
light of the experience of the priest in community and
his shamanistic roots.

THE SOURCE OF AUTHORITY

Fundamental to any theology of the priesthood is the source of its authority. For whom or what does the priest speak? A simple way to frame our response is to contrast the charismatic leader with the ordained leader or the internal call with the external call. The charismatic leader is one who responds to an internal call, as in some shamanistic religions. Ordination is the authorization of the priest by the community as described in the sociology of professions. Such authorization typifies the external call.

The charismatic notion of call derives its strength from humanity's concern for *how* we experience God. Such a call is a part of that personal inexpressible experience of God, for which it is the responsibility of the church to establish a climate where it might be heard. There is real truth in the charismatic notion of call, but it must be met in the other side by the obligation to say *what* we experience in God in order to judge the call's validity. The church is responsible for saying what that call is. Ordination is the seal of the church that it is true. In both the *how* and the *what* the church functions as the field of meaning, or *Gestalt*, for the experience of call.

This is why the Venice statement of the Anglican/ Roman Catholic International Commission, speaking on authority, started not with the hierarchy but with the church. The church is prior to everything but Christ, since the church is the primary sacrament of Christ.

We have every reason to be thankful for this new understanding of the church since World War II. It can be seen in the celebration of the Eucharist, which used to be a setting for private, individual devotion like the setting of a ring for some precious jewel. I recall in 1951 a friend of mine describing a Eucharist he had attended in an Episcopal parish noted for its excessive ultramontanism. He reported that during the prayer of thanksgiving a woman beside him was kneeling to say her rosary, the man in the pew in front of him was sitting reading an article in *The Holy Cross Magazine* entitled "Mary's Interests," a priest on the staff was hearing confessions in the rear of the church, and there was a constant procession of persons lighting candles before a well-advertised shrine of our Lady. I have had no reports of that particular parish since, but it is hard to imagine such activity on the American scene now. Our doctrine of the church makes clear the corporate nature of eucharistic worship. More people reading lessons, more opportunities for them to respond in liturgy, and the practice of passing the peace are symptomatic of this renewed emphasis on the centrality of the people of God in community.

As the primary symbol of Christ's presence in the world, all other expressions of the gospel flow from the church and the promise of Christ to be with her, including the priesthood. We do not *have* a community, we *are* our community. That consciousness of self, the peculiar possession of humankind, is the result of our socialization which enables us to transcend our biological destiny. It is by virtue of our community that we are more than our genotype or even phenotype. We are a Christian nootype—a people whose minds are formed by the tradition of Christ. Baptism into the people of God then becomes the entry into the illumination of a life lived in God and all that means for our future.

This is why in both contemporary Roman Catholic and Protestant theology the church is the mediator of salvation (wholeness) as given to us in Christ. The community of faith is the womb of faith. This is not to say that the institution of the church is perfect or that the individual is denied a certain sense of the immediacy of God. God uses the church, however, broken as it is: for the ministry, the sacraments, the scriptures, theology, the liturgy are meaningless save as they are rooted in that community. Our individual awareness of God is only made possible as the church points to where we might discover the presence of God and gives us the language with which to identify it, to interpret it, and to decide about it.

For example, we do not find God in the sunset until we have been nurtured in a community that knows God is Creator, that the Creator is good, and that there is a relationship between beauty and goodness. We "feel" the numinous, but we cannot "name" that feeling without the vocabulary of a community.

The call of priest, then, is a specific focus of what belongs preeminently to the priestly community. The New Testament does not know of a ministerial priesthood of any kind. Yet there is reference to the priestly community (1 Peter 2:5,9). As the ministerial priesthood evolved it was to act on behalf of the whole church as a means of illuminating what it means to be in Christ.

There could be no internal call without an external call by the church to this function. The external call is not simply to the professional model of the priest, for which one might apply, be accepted, trained, and certified to perform certain functions. The call to the priesthood is external in the sense that the priesthood is first the possession of the church and before the church it is the possession of Christ. Such understanding accords with the priest as the person onto whom the community projects the priestly image of the receptive mode of thinking that is rightly theirs. The priest embodies the meaning of the community becoming conscious of the experience of God. In this sense the priest is the symbol of the church's sacramentality as the primary symbol of Christ.

We miss an important point, however, if we dwell only on the church's validation of the external call as the source of the priest's authority. Very few people come to the priesthood because they have been "recruited" by the church. In fact, many a vocation exists in spite of the church. Of course, no one would recognize a call from God when he had one if it were not for the church, just as the church defines the terms for recognizing God in the sunset; but many priests do report a sense of having been singled out by God, even when the church gave little or no encouragement.

Certainly the church needs people to do certain things—preside at the Eucharist, pronounce absolution, give blessings—and it singles out some people to be given this job. In the early medieval European village the headman as often as not chose some son of the peasant class to be taught to say mass and to be ordained. The tradition in the English nobility of two hundred years ago was for the third son to seek orders. In a relatively stable, homogeneous society, with a clear sense of the place of "church," the devastating effect of such a system was not immediately apparent, as it would be today.

We know that ordination is not like the arranged marriage of dutiful children, obedient to the authority

of their families. The priestly ministry begins with an
internal call, perhaps like some shaman of old who
began at an early age to realize that somehow he was
"different." (Other shamans inherited the job from
their fathers.) Many people have fought that call for
years and that is good. The struggle itself begets a
natural selection process, which deepens commitment
for those who persist.

It would be tragic if the renewed sense of the people
of God as community appeared to question the priority
of the internal call to the priesthood, just as it would
be very unfortunate if a simplistic notion of charismatic experience failed to appreciate the necessity of the
church's ratification of such a call. The call is in fact
both internal and external because of the very nature
of what a priest must be to the community he serves.
The neo-Pentecostal movement has rightly recalled us
to an awareness that the Holy Spirit does seize our
lives and invite us into new ways of living, including
the work of the priest. If the priest is an "angel," a
messenger, it is as one from God. It is too much to
claim that the priest is only a messenger of the church.

This is a particularly sensitive truth to me as an
Episcopalian, as my denomination debates the so-
called clergy "surplus" and we reflect on the refusal of
a few dioceses to accept persons for ordination. Aside
from the fact that such prohibitions are statistically
short-sighted and occasionally misnamed (some dioceses mean by them that they are more selective than
before), these arbitrary refusals are theologically open
to question. This occurred to me when I heard a defense for them on the grounds that we do not understand the priestly community, and until we do we

should be very cautious about ordaining priests. My reply is that we will not understand the priestly community save in a reflection of the ministerial priesthood. The quest for understanding is not a linear explanation, but a dialectical search.

The source of the priest's call, and consequently his authority, is bimodal. The ministerial priesthood in the Christian church is not just an updating of the institutional Levitical priesthood of the old covenant. Parallels between the Christian and Levitical priesthoods have been claimed through the centuries. But the authority of the priest is related as well to the priesthood of Christ, which the author of Hebrews tells us has an integrity beyond the institution. "Thou art a priest forever, in the succession of Melchizedek" (5:6). Christ is not a priest by inheritance, much less as a result of applying for the job. Priesthood is an eternal, as well as internal, call from God independent of the tradition of the Israelite community.

The roots of priesthood go back far beyond the Christian church or the people of Israel into the prehistory of humankind, to the abyss from which our consciousness of ourselves before God springs. Melchizedek, who was probably a Canaanite priest-king, entertains Abraham, the father of the Judeo-Christian community, at a cultic meal and blesses him (Genesis 14:18–20). He emerges for a moment from the obscurity of human service to the ineffable God, to represent that primordial priesthood which bears little if any relationship to the action mode and structural definitions of the priest in Hebrew law, much less Christian institutions. He is a tantalizing image of the hero that lies on the edge of human consciousness, leading his community into an awareness of themselves before God, including an awareness of the priesthood, which is rightly theirs by birth and baptism. In the "eternal" priesthood Melchizedek is the embodiment of the universal archetypical priestly image in human consciousness.

So what does this mean for the source of the authority of the priest? For whom does he speak?

The priest speaks *to* the church for the God who speaks to the soul of every individual and community. The priest speaks *for* the church to the church and the world. His call is both internal and external, both of the receptive mode and the action mode. If psychologist Julian Jaynes is right and the receptive mode of thinking is the locus of God speaking to us, then the individual is called by God in that mode of consciousness. It may be dramatic, it may be very subtle, but it is internal. Yet that is not sufficient in itself. We are not shamans, practicing on our own. We are members of the community of faith, who in our ministry represent that community. Therefore, our internal call must be examined and ratified by the community in the action mode. This is an act of discerning the Spirit. The community must ask: Is this call of God? That is what I mean by the external call: the reflective examination of the experience of a call and its felt meaning.

The authority of the priest comes, therefore, both from God and the church. The authority from God saves him from being a mere flunky of the institution and enables him to speak prophetically to the church, just as the ancient prophets in the Old Testament did to Israel. The authority of the church enables him to speak for the church, however, and to represent its priestly function both to itself and to the world.

PRIESTLY CHARACTER

But what is the guarantee of that bimodal authority? This raises the historic issue of "character." Character has a special meaning, as to priesthood (as well as baptism); it bears looking into here. It is derived from a Greek word meaning the imprint of a wax seal or the die used to stamp coins. St. Augustine of Hippo used it to counter the Donatist heresy, which claimed that the efficacy of a sacrament is affected by the internal or moral disposition of the priest. It still has relevance, despite the fact that character has official status only in the formularies of the Roman Catholic Church since the Council of Trent. In the canons of that sixteenth-century council it is said that these sacraments convey "character": baptism, confirmation, and orders. Its relevance lies in the fact that many Christians are still Donatists and, therefore, the problems to which St. Augustine spoke still remain.

Anyone who has served in authority over priests knows in what sense Donatism still lives. For if the sins of a priest, particularly the "warm sins" relating to passion, gain notoriety among the people in our moralistic society, the cries for the blood of the priest flood the mails, the appointment calendar, and the telephone of him who is responsible for that priest's future. Probably our society responds so strongly to the "warm sins" because we suffer from what Jung would call a corporate "anima-possession." We have suppressed the feminine within our masculine corporate self-image out of fear for the Great Mother in us all, and this is the way she "gets" us.

In one such tragic situation I recall being told "to cast the money changer out of the temple"—which

still strikes me as a most curious bit of exegesis. But
the most frequent query in the face of notorious (in the
eyes of the scandalized) sin on the part of a priest is:
"How can you expect me to receive communion from
his hands?"

Such a question reveals a Donatist doctrine of the
priesthood; namely, that the effectiveness of the priest
is contingent upon his freedom from sins. In the ancient church the sins were murder, apostasy, and adultery, a very narrowly conceived catalogue. We might
probably drop apostasy today and add a few, such as
indiscriminate compassion and bad taste.

Of course, the obvious chink in the Donatist's armor
is his understanding of what constitutes sin, that is, the
narrowness of the catalogue. No one, including the
priest, is free of sin. More often than not our sins are
more insidious and destructive than those resulting
from excessive passion. It is the "cold" sins of gossip,
moral blindness, meanness of spirit, and the like that
disturb me far more. If the existence of sin calls into
question the effectiveness of the sacraments over
which a priest presides, then it would be unreasonable
to receive any sacrament from the hands of any priest.
Yet notorious sin does scandalize the faithful and that
must be taken into account.

The church since St. Augustine has struggled to live
with the fallibility of its priests and the sensitivity of
its people by distinguishing between *validity* and
fruitfulness. Validity is an action mode concept that
spares us from having to know the moral inner intention of the priest in order to be guaranteed the authority of his office. It rests the question of the symbolic
reality of a sacramental action upon the interaction between the priest and those he serves, and not on the
priest's internal disposition. The sins of the priest

aside, God is present to those who engage the validly ordained priest in faith, both within the liturgy and in his extra-liturgical ministrations. That assurance relates to what theology has come to call priestly "character."

Before examining character further, however, we need to touch on what fruitfulness means, lest the notion of character suffer the caricature common to theological polemics. In the theological concept of character a priest is not a sacramental "automat." The style of his life can make a difference. It is entirely reasonable to remove a priest who by his style of life scandalizes his people and causes their faith to "stumble." This removal would not be because his ministry is invalid, but because it is not fruitful. Fruitfulness is related to the receptive mode. What a priest is or does may obscure the proclamation, the word of God fundamental to the priestly ministry. The mirror of projection is so obscured and blurred that it is not even a "puzzling reflection" or "enigma" (1 Cor. 13:12). But it is not his sins which render him an ineffective symbol, but the unfruitful effect his sins have on our faith.

This negative effect can vary from time to time and person to person. I find little evidence, for example, that a tenth-century French priest who kept a concubine and raised numerous children was rendered ineffective in the average tenth-century French village. In most contemporary communities he would not last forty-eight hours. In small-town America a priest of dominantly homosexual orientation cannot function, no matter what his actual social practices. In our larger cities he can have a very effective ministry. So the fruitfulness of the priest is relative to the subjective consciousness of those to whom he ministers.

Character is absolute, however, and liberates us

from the bondage of subjectivism. It defines that condition which, once it is established, exists irrespective
of our feelings toward the other person, whether of
attraction or revulsion. It is my observation that whatever we may call it, the reality to which character points
exists in the relationship of the priest to the community
even among those who repudiate the theology of sacramental character. For even when Protestant denominations depose their clergy for moral turpitude,
reinstatement generally does not involve reordination.
Whatever it is Protestant clergy possess by virtue of
their initial ordination they retain despite disciplinary
action by the community. When in the Episcopal
Church the ordination of women was finally approved,
there was no overwhelming effort to demand that the
women already ordained without official consent of the
community go through ordination again, presumably
because they already possessed the character of priesthood by virtue of the irregular ordination.

This indelibility of priestly character is found in the
internal call and the roots of the priesthood in the receptive mode. Once the priestly image has fallen upon an
individual it "haunts" him. As for the "whiskey priest"
in Graham Greene's *The Power and the Glory* and my
father's colleague who pled with me not to lose my
faith, the priesthood is like the stigmata in the hands
and feet of the risen Christ. They remain despite all.

Once this has been said of character, it may be even
further defined. Three possibilities arise from history.

There is, first, the ontological definition of character.
This interpretation depends upon a naive realism.
Naive realism holds that human nature exists substantially, apart from the accidents of birth and what that
means for our genetic history (the genotype) and of our

community and what that means for our socialization
(the phenotype). Furthermore, human nature is
thought to exist apart from the knowing subject. For
naive realism human nature is a thing "out there,"
independent of history. The baptismal service in the
1928 Book of Common Prayer reflects this same notion, where the whole tone of the service implies a
transplant of one human nature in place of another.
The service seems to say that there is the human nature which cannot participate in the Kingdom of God
and, presumably, there is the regeneration of that one
which may participate.

The ontological definition of character says that the
human nature of the individual priest is changed by
ordination, as a scientist in the future might correct a
genetic defect with a laser beam. "Character is a distinctive mark," St. Thomas Aquinas is reported to have
said, "printed on a man's rational soul by the eternal
Character Christ Himself . . . distinguishing the man
from those who are not so likened according to the
state of faith." The "rational soul" is, according to
Aquinas, the distinctive nature of humankind. This
theory would have real possibilities if we accepted the
existence of a substantial human nature or rational
soul. Most theologians today do not accept it.

A second definition of character is moral or covenantal. This approach arose in the history of the
church when naive realism was being challenged and
the notion of a substantial human nature refuted. The
argument was that there is no essential or necessary
reality which makes individual persons "human," but
only the fact that we consider them human. Covenantal character taught that in ordination God promises
the priest that whenever he presides in accordance

with the practice of the church at the Eucharist God will be present. The priest's response to this promise, which makes it a true covenant, is his acceptance of the discipline of the priesthood. Character is then a promise of God, like the pledge we might make to give more money to our parish church.

The covenantal definition of character has been criticized as weak. It does not seem to coincide with the experience of a priesthood that can survive and grow in spite of the violence done the office by those who embrace the priesthood. Its external quality does not correspond to the internal reviviscence of ordination. It is noteworthy that the fifteenth-century "father" of the covenantal or moral theory, Gabriel Biel, was an influence on Martin Luther, who ridiculed the notion of character, apparently having no strong feeling for what it describes in our experience.

A stronger definition of character, which avoids as well the naive realism of the ontological view, is sociological. Its strength depends upon our understanding that the human person is more than what lies inside his skin, but that the self is the community in which the person was born and is nurtured. Thus defined character is the role which society expects of us and, most important, which we as a result expect of ourselves. We are defined in all kinds of ways by the society which claims us, and this definition becomes our own. Within the community of faith there are a few clearly distinguished sets of expectations. Baptism marks one, ordination another.

Character, then, by this definition is the community's identification of a person as priest, confirmed by its response to him in this office. Character does not pertain to an individual's substantial human nature, since we do not know what that is, if it is. But character is more than simply a morally binding agreement. It is the nature of the interaction between the priest and the people served. It points to the primordial reality of human existence, where the hero leads the community into a consciousness of what it is to be human before the Creator. As Karl Rahner writes, "Priestly ordination gives once and for all a very definite, permanent assimilation to Christ and a social connection with him as head of the Church, and hence assigns him his place in the social organism of the Church."

In the previous section I suggested that the priesthood of Christ leads more directly to understanding the ministerial priesthood than the Old Testament Levitical priesthood. The priesthood of Christ leads us beneath a simple equation of priest with the traditional sacrificial cultic figure. Christ is the means of God's self-disclosure or revelation. He images for us what it is to be human before God. This is a priestly act, while at the same time it is a prophetic act. To possess priestly character is to accept the expectation of the church to mediate this word of revelation in Christ. The community of faith expects to be illuminated by the priest, and that expectation, and its fulfillment in Christ, is priestly character.

This expectation was brought home to me very clearly in the survey of parish calling committees in the Episcopal Church made in 1974–75, which I cited in the fourth chapter. We asked these committees what they valued most highly in a prospective priest. They answered that the personal quality they wanted most was spiritual depth and the skill they wanted was one of preaching effectively. Both of these, spiritual depth and skilled preaching, are means of illumination in Christ.

THE PREREQUISITES OF VALIDITY

If priestly character is the place of the priest in the social organism as one assimilated to Christ, the light of the world (John 1:4–9,8:12), then the knowledge of the truth or validity of that character in some sense rests with the church. It is analogous to a company hiring an executive. If the executive is to perform a certain function in the company, then the company must set the criteria for the appointment so that it may be seen as binding. A sacrament is valid if it does not have to be repeated. In classical sacramental theology the terms of the knowledge of the validity of a sacrament such as holy orders are the proper matter, form, intention, subject, and minister. Who determines what is proper? The fantasy of many devout church people is that Christ and/or the scriptures lay out the proper matter, form, intention, subject, and minister. The fact is, as history shows and this approach argues, that the church is the final judge of what is proper.

Some may insist, however, that the New Testament spells all this out. It is true, in a few instances. The scriptures, for example, tell us that the matter of baptism is water and of the Eucharist bread and wine. But it says nothing certain about the form or words which should accompany the matter. It is probable that baptism, for example, was in the name of Jesus at first (Acts 2:38) rather than the Trinity. We do not know what the first prayers of thanksgiving in the Eucharist were, except that they were improvised by the president. There is a distinction that we need to make between the symbolic reality of the sacrament, what the sacrament does, and the rite by which that reality is shared. The symbolic reality is found in the assurance of God's presence, his grace given to us; but the rite, with its matter, form, intention, subject, and minister, sensible to that symbolic reality, are the domain of the church.

I need to note briefly what I mean by "sensible to the symbolic reality," because I will return to it. When the scriptures clearly specify the matter of a sacrament, such as water in baptism, it would not be sensible to the symbolic reality to substitute rose petals. When there is a tradition as old as the fourth century that the priest presides at the Eucharist, it would not be sensible to the symbolic reality suddenly to confer that right upon deacons. I personally do not think it would be sensible to the symbolic reality present in holy matrimony to permit the subjects/ministers of that sacrament to be two parties of the same sex, although I have no problem about the blessing of any friendship. To be sensible to the symbolic reality is to do nothing to obscure the church's intended effect for the participant in that sacrament.

What is clear is that we must be very cautious in claiming too much for one view of the prerequisites for the knowledge of a valid ordination. It is up to the church.

The *matter* for ordination is the laying on of hands. From the eleventh century until modern times, however, the bestowal of the instruments, the chalice and paten, were considered the matter of ordination. The Council of Florence (1438–45) declared it dogma. Hardly anyone would say this now, and we have gone back to the imposition of hands. Yet it still may change again. A Roman Catholic theologian has recently suggested that a simple declaration by the Pope can render someone a priest. The important thing is that this be a public act of ordination so the people may ratify the call.

The *form* for ordination is a personal and then later a community composition. Arguments over the form generally relate to the intention expressed or not expressed by the form. No doubt the change in the form for ordination of a priest in the 1552 Book of Common Prayer was adopted with this in mind. In the form the church expresses what it believes the symbolic reality is which the sacrament effects. In the ordination it is to make a priest.

The *intention* is the imponderable aspect of validity, since it is the subjective element in the sacrament. It seeks to answer the question: In participating in a sacrament what does the church intend to do? There is no way of getting at this very slippery issue in a final sense among participants, at a given moment in history. This is why a true intention is described as intending only what the church intends, even if we do not know what that is or appear outside the rite to intend something else. A minister of a sacrament can disavow publicly whatever he wants, but as long as the intention of his actions in presiding at the rite is the same as that of the church the intention of the sacrament is considered valid.

This is the only way we can be free from the caprice of subjectivism. There was an Anglican bishop in the nineteenth century who customarily before every ordination said in his remarks to the ordinands. "I do not intend to ordain sacrificing priests." But by using the rite of the church this bishop affirmed his intention to do what the church intends, and therefore his opinions about sacrifice and the Eucharist were irrelevant. Furthermore, by employing that rite he relates to the receptive mode of meaning which is operative no matter what statements he makes in the action mode.

If the question of intention seems very fuzzy it is because it is fuzzy. This is why in 1896, when it was politically expedient for the Roman Catholic Church to repudiate Anglican orders for the sake of the Roman Catholics in England and the United States, they chose to attack the intention of the Anglican ordinal. Intention is the "quicksand" of any sacramental theology. What Pope Leo XIII had to say then is capable of at least seven possible interpretations, none of which is really convincing.

The *minister* of ordination is the bishop. But again, this is because the church says he is. As a matter of history, in the third century the bishop and patriarch of Alexandria was ordained bishop by presbyters, as best we can tell. John Wesley argued for the validity of Methodism's presbyteral ordination on the basis of this precedent. In the fifteenth century an abbot in priests' orders at the appointment of the Pope ordained other priests. Recently Edward J. Kilmartin has claimed that we know that an ordination is valid just so long as the proper authority in the ecclesial body so states, by whatever official authority or means desired. The validating act is the prescribed designation of the community, not the title of the person or the nature of the act. This seems quite consistent with the bimodal source of the priest's authority.

Each term of knowing the validity of ordination has been debated within the church at particular times in history. Anglicanism in the 1970s is particularly caught up in the debate over the proper *subject*. Who can be ordained? At its most limiting point the church said only baptized males without visible physical defect. In other words, if you were heathen, female, or blind you were not a fit subject. It was the church that made that decision, some would say by clear inference from the scriptures. Yet no one now considers physical defects final impediments, although in the Roman Catholic Church one must still get a dispensation to ordain someone who is deaf or missing a leg, for example. The debate over subjects now centers on whether females are proper subjects.

Because the sexual symbols are so heavily charged and bring us so quickly to the edge of our personal abyss, there has always been a tendency to ground this aspect of the knowledge of validity in some notion of human nature. It seems too risky to trust this to the church and history. Not only is this inconsistent, of course, with sacramental theology, it does violence to what we understand about the nature of priesthood in the community and the meaning of baptism. Yet the appeal to nature occurs, as ignorant as it is.

In seminary we called this the "teddy bear" argument. One of the standard questions on sacramental theology went as follows: If some children are playing church and they baptize their teddy bear, is the teddy bear a baptized Christian? The question is obviously absurd because everyone knows that sacraments are for humans and teddy bears are not human. But those who argue that by nature women cannot be ordained are saying the same thing. The clear implication is that women are not human as men are human; they are teddy bears.

This is not to say that this is the only argument against the ordination of women to the priesthood. There are those who speak with more cogency of the sensibility to the symbolic reality; but that leads us to the next section. But first it is clear that it is the church which decides the marks by which we determine the

validity of ordination. The community of faith is prior
to all other expressions of the gospel. This is consistent
with the contention that the priest belongs to the
people of God as the symbol who evokes for them
through their projections the knowledge of the presence of God that is within the community and within
each of us.

THE SYMBOLIC REALITY

In the last section I frequently referred to sensibility
to the symbol reality. The phrase "symbol reality" is
equivalent to what in classical sacramental theology
was called *res et sacramentum*, "the thing and the
sacrament." It designates the effect of a rite. The effect
of ordination, for example, is priestly character. But
that priesthood is ultimately Christ's priesthood, and it
is this symbolic reality to which we need to be sensible. What does this mean?

Perhaps the keenest challenge to the ordination of
women to the priesthood lies in the speculation that
the priest is the *eikon*, or "stands for" Christ. The argument is "profound" not so much because it holds
water—the maleness of Jesus is not essential to God-
with-us—but because it opens the door to a considera-
tion of the relationship of Christ as the central, primordial symbol of God both to the church as the primary
symbol of Christ and to the priest as the evocative
symbol of the church's Christocentric reality.

The reader needs to remember that the priesthood—the ministerial priesthood or Christ's—is not to
be identified *merely* with cultic activity, as centuries of
theological debate have done. As stated in the first
chapter, to be a priest is to be a bridge builder, the

pontifex, between God and man, and to be initially rooted in the receptive mode of consciousness. The cultic representation of the sacrifice of Christ is the essential core of that bridge building, to which Christ's priesthood within the paschal mysteries is obviously related; but cult does not exhaust the illuminative function of the priest. Earlier in this chapter the point was made that to speak of Christ's priesthood as that of Melchizedek, the priest-king of Salem, was to evoke an image that gets us behind the cultic priesthood of the Israelite community. What is true of priesthood in general would be true of Christ's priesthood in particular. *The encompassing definition of its function is a salvific illumination.*

The clearest expression for the illuminative function is the minister of the Word. To speak of Christ as Word is to speak of him in a priestly, as well as prophetic, sense. Prophecy in the early church is ecstatic and apocalyptic. It seeks to unveil what God has in mind for us. Look at the juxtaposition of "Word" and "light" in the prologue of the fourth gospel. "The Word, then, was with God at the beginning, and through him all things came to be . . . . All that came to be was alive with his life, and that life was the light of men. The light shines on in the dark, and the darkness has never mastered it" (John 1:2–5). The Word illumines our darkness. Revelation provides additional commentary on the relation of the Word to Christ's priesthood. "Then I saw heaven wide open, and there before me was a white horse; and its rider's name was Faithful and True . . . he was robed in a garment spattered with blood. He was called the Word of God" (Revelation 19:11, 13). The imagery is of the Word, God-with-us, as the priestly messiah, spattered with blood as would be the high priest, conquering all that stands in the way of the final consummation, when all things shall be made light.

I dwell on the image of Christ's priesthood as the illuminating word because this is a touchstone of the relation of Christ to the ministerial priesthood. Karl Rahner says that the point of departure for determining the nature of the priestly office is as "proclaimer of the word of God." Rahner is by no means alone in this insistence that the service of the word is fundamental. Such proclamation finds its center in the Eucharist, where we proclaim Christ's death and resurrection until he comes.

But if the proclamation is one that illumines, as I have said, the act of illumination takes place in the contrast between the darkness of Good Friday and the light of Easter. We easily forget that light is dependent upon darkness and order upon chaos. To divide necessarily presupposes something to be divided. In our model of bimodality there can be no action mode without receptive mode and no receptive mode without the fathomless ocean. This raises a very interesting problem of defining Christ as *simply* the Word or, as I would prefer to say now in the original Greek, Logos.

The Logos is a concept common to the ancient philosophical world. It means *reason.* To a philosopher at that time, to say that God is mind was not to say he is consciousness with all that implies, but that he is *reasoning* consciousness. Furthermore, such a philosopher would insist that a person is like God in that he possesses a mind with a particle or seed of God's reasoning nature within him. *Reason is, of course, of the action mode, and this locates the image of God in that mode.*

Logos or reason identifies reality in its plurality. The action mode is analytical. Before reason can say what something is, it has to say what it is not. It sets one concept over against another. Logos therefore, divides. In Revelation the rider on the white horse, called the Word of God, has coming from his mouth a sharp sword (19:15). A sword divides. The Logos is that within each of us which drives us westward from the fathomless ocean to consciousness, and in so doing is a movement from unity to multiplicity. In a remarkable essay, Rahner points out that God in the movement outwards from himself in the gift of the Incarnate Word informs our consciousness and yet shifts from unity to multiplicity.

Sometimes professors can become blinded by the logic of their own thought. After all, our discipline is of the action mode. One summer I was teaching a seminar in advanced pastoral theology and a student wrote a long paper attacking knowledge. In its place he pled for understanding. The student, who characterized himself as a maverick Lutheran pastor, felt that all he had been taught in seminary was knowledge. I came to the defense of knowledge, only to learn later that the very distinction and criticism that this student made is also to be found in the thought of the German philosopher Heidegger, and that it makes precisely the point I am now making. Logos or reason seeks to control and, in so doing, divides. Understanding seeks to relate and, in so doing, unites.

There is a problem, then, in identifying the priesthood of Christ as Logos alone, just as there is a problem in the exclusive interpretation of Christ as Logos. The symbol leaves us divided. The Logos by itself is too much an action-oriented interpretation both of Christ's priesthood and ours. And so, as Rahner points our, we have to look for some key words to balance this logos-oriented notion of Christ, so loved by the Greek philosophers. We need a more bimodal interaction with Christ, so that it might inform our priesthood.

Rahner's answer to the problem is both helpful and unhelpful. He says the key words are the Sacred Heart of Jesus, "designating the Lord as him who brings the one and the all into unity, and which in turn unifies and brings into man's interior soul the fulness of him whom it designates in this sense." The image of the Sacred Heart of Jesus, as I mentioned in passing in an illustration in the second chapter, is a central aspect of Roman Catholic folk religion. It is a felt, feminine meaning breaking through the rational, masculine action mode of consciousness in Christianity. So Rahner's introduction of the Sacred Heart is highly provocative—perhaps more so than he realizes. Yet I would prefer to go with another key word or image rather than the Sacred Heart. This is Eros. Eros is a sensible word, less overlaid with the sentimental piety of seventeenth-century French ladies than the Sacred Heart or the contemporary Protestant version of the Sacred Heart, the portraits of a simpering, sweet Jesus.

In spite of the constant efforts to trivialize Eros, in pictures of chubby cupids, or to pervert it, as in equating erotic with pornographic, Eros speaks to that infinite emptiness that longs to be filled by the Other, culminating in the infinite fullness of God. Eros is the desire for oneness. It connotes harmony and synthesis. Mythologically it has always been conceived as a joining of masculinity and femininity into one complete being. Analytical psychology calls such a whole person the androgyne, a term which we have already related to the priest.

To speak of androgynes conjures up to some people

thoughts of sexual freaks, although the word is not used to denote the same phenomenon as the hermaphrodite. Androgyny has to do with consciousness, not anatomy. It describes knowledge, understanding, and even more. To be human is to be whole, which means our rational selves and not just our intuitive selves. But even more, we must face toward that to which the receptive mode points: chaos. The whole person also acknowledges the abyss within. If we deny the abyss, if we refuse to leap in faith into the abyss as the shaman of old or, as some may recall, Carlos Castaneda does at the end of his book *Tales of Power,* both the receptive and the action mode have no word of the living God.

If Christ is Logos, then Christ is also Eros, and abyss, because he is fully human. This is not something we would think ancient philosophy could say, with its excessively rational concept of God that protected it from the dark mysteries of Eros and chaos.

Yet in the writings of the fourth-century St. Gregory of Nyssa, particularly in the *Fifteen Homilies on the Canticle of Canticles,* we find a repeated discussion of Eros and the darkness as the necessary conditions for humanity's assimilation with the Godhead. This, combined with Gregory's discussion of "sober inebriation" as descriptive of the ecstasy the human spirit experiences in the presence of God, points to a profound appreciation of the receptive mode in the ascetical life. For Gregory, who prized chastity as much as anything, Eros is the love that overwhelms humankind in God's self-revelation. It follows inevitably that Christ is, as the agent of divine self-disclosure, Eros.

What for Gregory thwarted the realization of the goal of Eros, the assimilation with the Godhead, was *pathos,* "passion," particularly sexual passion. As bril-

liant as Gregory was, he was still a child of that particular, exclusively masculine stage of the evolution of
human consciousness typical of the fourth century.
Anders Nygren, the contemporary Swedish theologian, is no more insightful, however, in his attack upon
Gregory and Eros in his study *Agape and Eros*. Inexplicably, he misunderstands Gregory and takes him
to task for thinking that human love can bring man to
perfection. The best contemporary revision of Gregory's insight as to the importance of Eros is found in
the work of Rollo May, who knows that Eros can go
astray but yet is the power of wholeness. Eros has its
demonic side, which is not simply sexual passion but a
perversion of such passion. The light and the darkness
always appear together.

As Gregory intuitively knew, we should be aware
that what Logos divides Eros must unite. Eros
brings humankind back to the primordial unity of life
found at the edge of the abyss. It is that drive to oneness of which St. Augustine spoke in the *Confessions:*
the restless heart that seeks God, the One. Eros is the
channeling of the energy from the abyss for the purpose of integration and transformation. Nonetheless,
Eros must have Logos to protect us from the demonic
possibilities of Eros.

Eros as the feminine symbol is the mystagogue
which leads us to God. In the Christian tradition the
prototypical woman, the new Eve, the embodiment of
the feminine symbol, the Blessed Virgin Mary, is
theotokos. She is the "bearer of God" to humankind.
The Blessed Virgin epitomizes the power of that symbol in all our experience. Charles Williams, Christian
novelist, poet, and editor, in reflecting upon the figure
of Beatrice in Dante's *Divine Comedy*, points out that

the generic woman is *theotokos*. Dante, when he first
saw the nine-year-old Beatrice, trembled as one
drawn into the abyss. The feminine provokes such
sweet terror, which we must not allow an excessively
masculine, action-oriented theology to thwart. This
feminine Eros, guarded by Logos, must be, then, a
part of that symbolic reality which the priest conveys
if he is to be one who illumines the life of the community as *theotokos*, the symbol and the symbol bearer of
God.

Earlier I quoted the lyrics of Johnny Cash, which
reveal an insight not altogether common in the church.
Dory Previn, another spokesman for our introspective
age, has written some equally insightful if more enigmatic lines, which include these that call to mind the
coincidence of opposites in the image of Christ as
Logos and Eros.

> Jesus was an androgyne,
> Jesus was a he and she;
> Jesus was a freako, baby,
> Just like you and me.
> Jesus was a pagan,
> Jesus was a priest;
> Jesus was a beauty,
> Jesus was a beast.

The coincidence of Logos and Eros is a model for
bimodal consciousness. It is a key for the understanding of the priest in community because, as Dory Previn says, it is a model for you and me. Logos as the
masculine symbol and Eros as the feminine symbol
speak eloquently of the symbolic reality of ordination.
But she tells us "Jesus was a beast." Is this simply a

play on the fairy tale of "Beauty and the Beast," or does the fairy tale itself point to the possibility of which Aristotle was aware: that outside the city humanity is either a beast or a god? Indeed she suggests that the darkness from which light and reason are divided is a possibility (a temptation?) of the Christ. This is indeed a mystery, but it is also a reality of humanity's awareness embodied in Christ. In our center there is darkness and our very self is grounded upon that mystery which the darkness enshrouds.

The priesthood of Christ is the priesthood of Logos, of Eros and the abyss: the mediation of both a clear consciousness of God's purpose, which answers our longing to know as we are known, and a union with the divine presence, which satisfies our deepest craving to be consumed by the love of God. Both emerge from the abyss out of which God speaks to humanity. The coincidence of Logos and Eros makes it possible for us to follow both the scholar and the mystic who stands ultimately in ignorance before the mystery of the ineffable God. Such a priesthood is the symbol of the many, the one, and pregnant nothing. The priest in the church is called to serve this priesthood of Christ, to stand in the midst of the cloud of unknowing, to lead the community to the consciousness of God's saving word, and to invite into God's strengthening arms those who are far from his presence.

SUMMARY

There is no doubt that this chapter develops a more subtle theology of the priesthood than was promised in the illustrations of the earnest demeanor of the Mormon missionaries and the moving words of Johnny

Cash. But then my intent is more subtle because the insight is easier to lose than what the Mormons or even Johnny Cash intend to share.

Someone who has read most of what I have written once said to me that while he was bothered by my unusual beginnings he was relieved that I usually ended up orthodox. I suspect it might also be said of me what Dom Gregory Dix once said of certain neo-orthodox theologians. They are the more dangerous because they use the familiar language to mean something very different. Actually I think both statements would be true of what I have said in this chapter and this book.

What I am seeking in this study, to use the term of the French philosopher Paul Ricoeur, is a "second naiveté" of the symbol of the priest. Second naiveté is the post-critical or contemporary equivalent of the ancient or pre-critical immediate manifestation of the holy. Because most of humankind no longer testifies to seeing the "burning bush" that Moses, a pre-critical man, saw (Exodus 3:2–4) does not mean the bush is not there. We can only arrive at it, however, through a critical interpretation. We cannot regain the innocence we lost. We can only go forward. We believe so we understand, and yet we must understand so we can believe, both at the same time.

The experience of second naiveté requires that we suspend all previous interpretations and go to the heart of the symbol, in this case the priest. Then we must reinterpret. In moving from symbol to thought we can often see why those theologians who went before us spoke as they did. Their words are still meaningful. But we also discover that their words were shaped by their times and its ideological commitment.

If the theology of the priesthood as I have defined it
does not refer at all times to the same interpretation, it
is because this is not the fourth, or the thirteenth, or
the sixteenth century.

Whatever we say about the priest must not limit him
to the point where the power that belongs to that office
is suppressed. More than one commentator on Christianity has pointed out that the priest has become a
source of repression and guilt instead of ecstasy and
wonder because of our need to keep him in the action
mode for the sake of control. What greater privilege is
there than to be a symbol of that consciousness within
each of us that lies so close to God's word in the receptive mode?

Not so long ago I was sent a letter, found in the files
of my childhood priest, written by the wife of the
headmaster of the school from which I was to graduate
four years later. She was inquiring about me, who had
just applied to enter the school. "He really sounds a
bit queer—not yet 13 and six feet tall," she remarked.
"He wrote such a sophisticated letter and stated that
he intended becoming a priest of the church since the
age of 11." That is a bit "queer." "Queer" it undoubtedly was! But is any explanation at any age for wanting
to enter the priesthood any less queer, any less incon-
gruous to a world that is comfortable only with the
obvious?

Perhaps no one was more instrumental in cementing
my puerile call than the chaplain at that very school.
He was delightfully weird. When I was only just past
my thirteenth birthday and still on the way to a termi-
nal height of six feet, six inches, each week he had me
kneeling in the dawn before the altar of a small chapel.
It was a crazy thing to be doing in the eyes of the

ordinary world. More often than not the priest and I were the only ones there—shades of medieval oratories! The chapel was cold and the flagstones hurt my knees. I have never fainted in church, but I came closest there. Yet somehow in the dim candlelight, serving a Eucharist I little understood, I knew that the priest and I were doing something wonderful. It was a delicious moment, utterly removed from the routine of school or any other place. Here, in a primordial world, where God was so close it seemed I could reach out and touch him, I knew a certain illumination which remains with me today. I only hope that that priest of so long ago may read these lines and know of my abiding gratitude.

- *APPENDIX* -

Implications for Theological Education

MY mother was given to reminding me from time to time that "you can't make a silk purse out of a sow's ear." I was never certain whether my mother was letting me down easy or if this was part of her own way of handling disappointed expectations. I do know that it has served me in the latter sense as I have struggled with preparing persons for ordination to the priesthood. No one would wish to be known as "a sow's ear," but this study does force upon us the reality of the different capacities of individuals—capacities with which, I suspect, we are born or develop very early in life. What does this mean for theological education?

It takes more than good education to develop effective priests. This study reveals subtleties in the priestly symbol that are not readily transferable to curriculum design. Further, the priest is to occupy more

than a professional role. Consequently, while education plays a vital role in shaping the potential in a
likely candidate for the priesthood, notions about professional education do not exhaust the implications for
the development of effective priests.

There has always been some form of preparation for
ordination, however, if nothing more than memoriza-
tion of the Latin mass. Seminary education in America in the form we know it, except among Roman
Catholics, traditionally consists of three formal years of
training, but this pattern is no more than one hundred
seventy-five years old. It came into being as a result, at
least in part, of a growing apprehension over the
secularization of higher education in this country. It
was more a reaction than an intentional, active effort to
understand the priesthood and then accordingly design ways of producing such priests. This reaction was
rooted in the excessively action-mode-oriented assumptions of the post-sixteenth-century church. The
assumption was that one becomes a good Christian—
and, presumably, an effective priest—by assimilating
and regurgitating "Christian information." A caricature—and not one too exaggerated—would be able to
recite the books of the Bible, the seven deadly sins, the
offices of instruction from the 1928 Book of Common
Prayer, the seven sacraments, and the heresies at the
first ecumenical councils as a way of proving one had
mastered the Bible, moral theology, liturgics, theology,
and church history. In this theory, if a person can learn
the information and communicate it he can be an effective priest.

In the Episcopal church, as well as others, there is
clear evidence that this assumption is being challenged. In the canon law of my tradition, for example,

it is required of seminaries that they not only report to a candidate's bishop his academic performance, but also an evaluation of his personal qualities. Clinical Pastoral Education, an important part of theological education, judges the emotional character of the student as a potential pastor. This opens—albeit cautiously—the question of the person's awareness of receptive thinking.

The personal qualities of an individual—e.g., his imagination, creativity, empathy, stability, spiritual depth, humility, and sensibility—are hard enough to measure and report. It is next to impossible to conceive of how they may be taught where they do not exist. Such persons cannot be "created"; they have to be found. Therefore, the shift away from an *exclusive* academic evaluation toward a more personal and internal judgment has fostered interest in the selection of proper candidates for the priesthood. It is true you cannot "make a silk purse out of a sow's ear." If a person does not possess at least latent qualities such as we believe are both desirable and necessary for the effective priest, then he should never be sent to seminary.

The word "exclusive," however, can lead to an unfortunate polarity. We tend to see things as either/or rather than both/and. If the academic preparation of a priest is not the only basis upon which we can predict effective service, we must frequently defend the idea that intensive academic preparation has no validity at all. This charge is supported by a persistent and growing anti-intellectualism in many Christian congregations.

For example, at the seminary I serve our records show that if an applicant makes less than 500 on the verbal scale in the Graduate Record Examination he will probably have academic trouble. With less than 400 he is highly likely to fail academically. In selecting students we take this into account and consequently fall under persistent criticism from those who suggest that a vocation is not judged by the score on the Graduate Record Examination. This protest seems reasonable, but, as a matter of fact, the Graduate Record Examination is the most reliable piece of "hard data" we have for predicting success not only in seminary, but often after ordination. We find that when students did poorly academically but were let by because they seemed so "committed" they generally had a disastrous ministry.

When we ignore the conceptual skills identified with the action mode and consequently misconstrue the criterion of bimodal consciousness for ourselves and future priests, we grow sentimental. We become victimized by our feelings. This is happening with great frequency in the Episcopal Church. In 1975, thirty-five per cent of all the persons preparing for ordination to the priesthood in the Episcopal Church were doing so outside of accredited seminaries. This is in spite of the fact that the Episcopal Church is ordaining more priests than it seems to think it can use. There is no reason to believe that figure has diminished since 1975. Other denominations are more successful at resisting this sentimental interpretation of what makes an effective priest, but their past record has not always been that good.

Generally what training that thirty-five per cent receives is a pale imitation of the "informative factories" of our accredited seminaries a generation ago. There is no serious attention to personal formation, which requires constant confrontation in a primary community. It is sometimes argued that spiritual formation takes place because they worship together. Corporate worship is altogether commendable and necessary, but it is not in itself formation.

The trend away from intensive, accredited theological education is sometimes justified on the grounds that we need to identify and ordain the indigenous priest in a given community. What I have said about the shamanistic roots of the priesthood would appear to lend support to this argument. I have been told that theological seminaries "ruin" persons for being effective priests in remote, small, and less educated communities. The reader may wonder, then, why I insist that the trend away from accredited theological education is a serious error. My answer is what I have said in this study: the effective priest must be truly bimodal. *It is no better to live exclusively in the receptive mode than to confine oneself to the action mode.*

To switch the metaphor from a silk purse to gold— perhaps more appropriate in a book that makes positive use of the alchemical tradition—one cannot make gold out of lead or any other base mineral. If one wants gold, what a person must do is search for gold ore, which then may be refined into gold. Not every rock has the potential of becoming twenty-four-carat gold. We need to learn to find the gold ore, but then the refining is equally necessary. We need then to develop the best ways of refining the gold. To do this we must have some idea of what gold looks like.

This book is an effort to describe what the priest looks like. Undoubtedly there are those who believe "with God all things are possible," and as long as one truly thinks God has chosen him as a priest all personal problems can be overcome. In the terms of the metaphor, everyone is gold ore. This belief runs contrary to everything we know about God's way with humanity. God works through, not around, our human limitations. If we know what a priest is, we know that only a few within the community have the gifts to serve effectively in that function. This is why selection, not curriculum, is the first and last word in effective preparation of persons for the priesthood. If the notion of selectivity worries us, it may be because we think—consciously or unconsciously—that an ordained person is spiritually superior to the lay person. This, of course, is nonsense.

Granting the limitation on who can serve in theory, how do we make the theory operative? How are we sensible and not sentimental? In years as a university chaplain sending persons to seminary, as a member of seminary admissions committees, in writing evaluations, in conferring with diocesan officials, and as a seminary dean charged with telling students they are being dropped, I find the great difficulty in the identification of clear criteria. The claim to a vocation to the priesthood evokes a great deal of emotion, positive and negative, on the part of both the subject and those associated with him. This should be no surprise to the readers of this book. I personally have been accused of psychologizing, personal vendettas, secularism, and heresy in passing judgment upon candidates. Nowhere does sentimentality threaten sensibility more than here. The selection process, the finding of the gold ore, never stops during the refining process, but it is very hard sometimes to explain why, in one's own individual or corporate judgment, a student finally comes up "lead" rather than "gold."

Seminary faculty are often put in the position of being the villains in blocking the ordination of a person. It happens with a frequency that leads to the suspicion of collusion. Sentimental attachments to "our boy" back in his parish are devoid of a detached evaluation. To send someone to seminary is, let's be quite frank, a "feather in the rector's cap." I have seen applicants highly recommended by their parish priest whom anyone with an ounce of judgment would be sending to the psychiatrist, not to a seminary. This is a cruel truth. If we tell this truth, we can expect to receive the usual vilification. But, because of an inadequate vocabulary of judgment, the seminary's intuition is difficult to justify.

Diocesan bishops have more objectivity, although my experience is that diocesan boards—we call them commissions on ministry in the Episcopal church—are even more honest. At the diocesan level the tragedy of the person being ordained who is not capable of being effective is more obvious. Yet when a student is told that the seminary cannot foresee recommending him for ordination and, in some cases, is asked to leave, it is often very hard to explain to the bishops so that they understand why the seminary is taking such action. The reasons seem so general, and often more sinister explanations, sometimes fed by the home parish which also feels judged, may fester in the bishop's mind.

If we are going to guard against sentimentality we need to be able to describe what bimodal consciousness looks like. The search for identifiable, clear criteria for judging the potential of a person for the priesthood as that priesthood is described in this book lies in *the possibility for the differentiation* of certain character traits. Recall again the metaphor of the gold ore and the refined gold. True gold ore has the potentiality for the differentiation of the refined gold from what will become tailings, and this same judgment must be made of candidates for the priesthood. This is at the heart of the external call, as described in the sixth chapter.

Those character traits are interpersonal expressions of an intrapersonal integration, which reflect a person's ability to so understand his own inner life that he is free to function effectively as a priest in the community. If there is no realistic expectation that such intrapersonal insight will emerge, then such a person needs, for his own sake as well as the church's, to be rejected as a potential priest.

A beginning at defining such criteria, based on the fourth chapter, follows. In the left column are the categories and their descriptive traits which are appropriate to a helpful intrapersonal life. They all reflect a bimodal consciousness which begets a sensibility of interpersonal function. In the right column are those contraindicative traits, which appear to me to be strongly suggestive that there is no possibility for differentiation.

Differentiated Character Traits	*Contraindicative of Potential*
1. The Realistic Servant	
Humility	Self-righteousness
Humor	Staid-piousness
Self-forgetfulness	Egocentricity
Earthiness	Prudery
Vulnerability	Defensiveness
Self-esteem	Low self-image
2. The Servant of Change	
Flexibility	Rigidity

Love of solitude	Depression and loneliness
Insightfulness	Inexplicable anger
Clear sexual orientation	Asexuality
Courage	Fearfulness
Absolute faith, amid a plurality of belief	Heresy hunting
Tolerance of ambiguity	Intolerance and dogmatism
Awareness of the historicity of belief	Ideological fundamentalism

3. The Discerning Servant

Ability to conceptualize	Information gatherer
Spiritual detachment and distance	Emotional entrapment
Wide understanding and catholic taste	Narrow opinions and experience
Admission of ignorance	Pretense of knowledge
Compassion	Certitude
Command of feelings	Victim of feelings
A sense of injustice	Moral insensitivity

4. The Liminal Servant

Nonconformist, but interdependent	Conformist and dependent
Inner-directed	Outer-directed
Active passivity, a friend of death	Active for its own sake, particularly in the face of death
Contra-sexually aware	Sexually unaware
Errant, with style	Banal and/or dilettantish
Appreciation for symbol and story	Excessive intellectualization

5. The Authoritative Servant

Community-oriented	Status-oriented
Willing and able to manage	Manipulative
Responsible	Secretive

Decisive   Intimidated
Self-confident   Self-deprecating
Forgiving   Judging

Any such list as this is open to criticism, but I will claim a certain uniqueness for this one. It says nothing about the spirituality of the person, but everything in the left column demands a disciplined, deep spiritual life. Nothing is said about how intelligent someone must be. There is no question but that intelligence would greatly help in the emergence of these appropriate character traits. Obviously, no one possesses all the character traits in the left column. What is being described is a potential and a process, an ideal type (in the tradition of Max Weber, the great German sociologist). The question is whether there is the possibility of movement toward the left column in a candidate for the priesthood, or if there is a fixation in the traits listed in the right column making such movement very unlikely.

If we judge that a person possesses the potentiality, it is not possible as a rule to develop or refine that potentiality by anything but intensive theological education. The so-called "indigenous priest" is not discovered in a pure state. To treat him as if he were is grossly unfair to him, as well as the church.

At the same time, it is equally true that theological seminaries need to sharpen considerably their own sensitivity to the fact that their graduates have to function within a community, which is not a seminary. The seminary may easily bear no relationship to the community in which the priest must function after he graduates. We must be constantly sensitive to the *principle of transferability*. Our responsibility is to refine, not to destroy; and since the priest can only be the priest in community, to block the effectiveness of a candidate in the typical parish is to destroy the potential of a person as priest.

If the difficulty in selecting candidates for the priesthood on the part of congregations is sentimentality, the issue in seminaries is cynicism. The desire is, of course, for a bimodal sensibility in both. A few of the schools in which some clergy are trained, I must confess, destroy the product by their cynicism, because in effect they are graduate schools of religion and not communities for the formation of the priest. Their focus is on a field of inquiry, not on a community of faith. Undoubtedly such institutions are needed, but one wonders why they seek to train the parish clergy. They are occasionally staffed by persons either reacting to the sentimentality of the parish or escaping from the threat of pastoral encounters. If a faculty member has no involvement in a religious community, much less an interest in it, he can hardly model what such a life means.

Yet much more frequently the cause of cynicism within theological education, if it indeed exists at all, is the anti-intellectualism that persists in American religion. Seminary faculties are more often than not made up of persons with very deep, passionate commitments *which are expressed in their own intellectual inquiry.* This is difficult for people not a part of seminary life to understand, and faculty find themselves accused of lack of faith and unbelief. Students are sent to seminary with the admonition to resist the faculty, and excessive energy has to be expended breaking down the barriers erected by others. If there is just enough truth to this fiction to confirm the fears of those on a witch hunt, it is still anything but justified.

Such anti-intellectualism and careless caricature

beget much of the cynicism—some call it defen-
siveness—perceived in seminary faculties. It is like
beating a cur dog with a stick. If you do it long enough
he will stop licking your hand and will start biting.

There is no doubt that seminaries are rarified communities. This is a by-product of the necessary inten-
sity of their life. They must be introspective, which
means they are not always happy places. Carefully
weighed thinking and judicious responses are difficult
in such a charged atmosphere. Sometimes faculty
members have staked their professional careers on a
deep commitment to an insight which is not widely
shared, even if it is profoundly true. All of this can
generate a cloud of suspicion about "what goes on
there."

It is very hard when the question of what is going on
is posed to you as the proverbial: "Answer yes or no.
Have you stopped beating your wife?" One has to
guard carefully against the flip reply or the cynical curl
of the lip. This is particularly true at a time in the
history of the Episcopal church when there is no way
to answer which can make everyone happy. An explanation for the seminary faculty's position and/or action
would require the other person to undergo the same
educational process the faculty have experienced and
struggle day in and day out with the same community
issues the faculty now face. One can only fall back on
honesty and love and hope that the inquirer will accept the authenticity of the faculty's Christian faith.

This is to say that to overcome the cynicism of the
seminaries, real or imagined, there has to be trust between those in congregations and those in theological
education. On this we can then build a commitment to
the selection and education of persons capable of

being effective priests, acknowledging the inevitability of human error, but struggling toward a relatively well-defined goal. This requires sensibility, rather than either sentimentality or cynicism. I pray that this book can in some small way serve the establishment of such sensibility.